STRATEGY FOR LIVING

Edward R. Dayton
&
Ted W. Engstrom

Regal Books

A Division of GL Publications
Ventura, California, U.S.A.

Other good reading:
Be a Leader People Follow
by David C. Hocking
Living with Stress
by Lloyd Ahlem
A True View of You
by Stanley C. Baldwin
When the Going Gets Tough
by D. Stuart Briscoe

Rights for publishing this book in other languages are contracted by Gospel Literature International (GLINT) foundation. GLINT also provides technical help for the adaptation, translation, and publishing of Bible study resources and books in scores of languages worldwide. For further information, contact GLINT, Post Office Box 6688, Ventura, California 93006, U.S.A., or the publisher.

Fifteenth Printing, 1985

Published by Regal Books
A Division of GL Publications
Ventura, California 93006
Printed in U.S.A.

Code No. 54 034 05

Library of Congress Catalog Card No. 76-3935
ISBN 0-8307-0424-8

DEDICATION

To our wives,
who have often practiced
better than we have preached.

GOALS
Use what you have learned to decide . . . what it is God wants you to be and to do.

PRIORITIES
Discover which goals are more important.

PLANNING
Analyze the best way to reach your goals.

LIVING
Start working toward your goals according to your plans.

THE STRATEGY

- HOW WE LIVE OUR LIFE IS
    DETERMINED BY OUR **GOALS**

- WHAT GOALS WE CHOOSE ARE
    DETERMINED BY OUR **PRIORITIES**

- WHETHER WE REACH OUR GOALS IS
    DETERMINED BY OUR **PLANNING**

- A STRATEGY FOR **LIVING**
    NEEDS GOOD GOALS
    CHRISTIAN PRIORITIES
    EFFECTIVE PLANS

- IT IS IN THE LIVING THAT WE FIND
    BETTER GOALS
    HIGHER PRIORITIES
    MORE EFFECTIVE PLANS

- THE STRATEGY IS A **PROCESS**
    GOALS—PRIORITIES—
    PLANNING—LIVING

TRY IT! IT WORKS!

CONTENTS

Foreword **10**
To Those Who Helped **13**
How to Use This Book **14**

PART I The Strategy 17
Chapter 1 You Need a Strategy for Living **19**
But What of Life?/Not a Formula but a
Strategy/It's a Process
Chapter 2 How We Discovered the Strategy **25**

PART II Goals 29
Chapter 3 Goals Have Power to Change You **31**
Goals Are Motivators/We All Have Goals/
Understand Where You Fit
Chapter 4 You Need Goals to Live By **37**
Goals Help Us Psychologically/Goals Help Us
Physically/Goals Help Us Socially/Goals Help
Us Spiritually/Doing vs. Being/Why Are Some
People Afraid of Goals?

Chapter 5   Goals Give Purpose to Your Life   **47**
            Get Out of the Fog/A Goal Is a Measurable
            Purpose/Purposes vs. Goals/How to Write
            Good Goals/Relating Goals to One Another
Chapter 6   Put Your Goals to Work   **55**
            Seven Steps to Setting Goals/Tomorrow's Goals
            Impact on Today/But Is It Biblical?/Some
            Other Advantages of Goals/It's a Process

PART III Priorities 63
Chapter 7   How You Can Set Priorities   **65**
            When We Need Priorities/Choose the Future/
            Priority Questions/Putting It Together—the
            ABC's
Chapter 8   You Need to Make Decisions   **75**
            You Can Decide/Be an Initiator/Decisions Can
            Be Changed/It All Adds Up to Experience
Chapter 9   Priorities and Christian Commitment   **81**
            Priorities Have to Do With Values/The Three
            Levels of Christian Commitment/What About
            the Rest of My Life?

PART IV Planning 89
Chapter 10 You Need to Plan   **91**
            Planning Saves Time/What Is Planning?/Plans
            Are Changeable/Plans Help Communicate/
            Understanding God's Strategy/Planning Is like
            Problem Solving
Chapter 11 How to Do Personal Planning   **97**
            Describe Your Situation/The Case of the
            Lonely Husband/The Case of the "Crash
            Course" Manager/Planning *Is* like Problem
            Solving/The Case of the Concerned Mother/Is
            It Practical?/Do I Have to Replan?/Where Do
            You Get "Alternative Plans"?/Plan Time for

Planning/Use a "Things-to-Do" List/Big Plans,
Little Plans

PART V   Living   109
Chapter 12 Living All of Life   **111**
            Picture the Whole Person
Chapter 13 Living a Strategic Life   **119**
            Filling Empty Calendars/Time with God/Time
            with Your Spouse/Time with Your Family/
            Time for You/Time for Fellowship/Unplanned
            Time for Others/Time for Personal Planning/
            Time for the "Work"/Scheduling for Freedom/
            It's a Process

PART VI   Closing the Circle   131
Chapter 14 How to Set Goals for Your Life   **133**
            Here's How to Go About It/Suppose It Doesn't
            Work?/It's a Process/Everyone Should Do It
Chapter 15 Designing a New Life   **145**
            Things Are as They Are/Present
            Commitments/How Are You Spending Your
            Time?/What Does Your Time Inventory Say?/
            Look at Your Appointments/Comparing Goals
            to Practice/Analyzing the Results/Rebuild Your
            Goals/It's a Process
Chapter 16 Toward More Effective Living   **165**
            Develop a Standard Day/Consider a Standard
            Week/Family Planning Time/"Things-to-Do"
            List/Your Environment/Use Pareto's Principle/
            Discern God's Timing/Take Advantage of
            Delays/Use Strategy When You Shop/Have a
            Strategy for Cleaning the House/How
            Clergymen Misuse Their Time/Time Is Life
Chapter 17 Time Is Life   **175**
            Where Does the Time Go?/No One Has More

Time Than You/Be Successful/Time Seems to
Have Strange Qualities/Time Really Is but a
Measurement, a Dimension/Time Is Saved by
Discipline/Time Must Be Spent/Ask
Questions/Learn to Set "Posteriorities"/One
Thing at a Time

Chapter 18 You Have a Strategy for Living **183**
Set Goals/Establish Priorities/Make Plans/
Develop Schedules/Anticipate Problems/Utilize
New Information/Don't Be a "Time Nut"/And
Don't Be a "Goal Nut"/Control Your Time/
Plan for Life Planning

Bibliography **189**

FOREWORD

"Commit your work to the Lord, and your plans will be established" (Prov. 16:3, *RSV*).

Israel's wise men believed in planning. So did the greater Wise Man who taught His friends to count the cost of discipleship just as carefully as they would calculate the price of building a tall watchtower (see Luke 14:25-30).

Because Christian living is God's total demand on us, as well as His total provision for us, we cannot compartmentalize our commitments. Our time, our energy, our opportunities, our talents, our gifts, our relationships are all bestowed upon us by a gracious God. Nothing less than a strategy for Christian living is adequate response to such grace.

Ted Engstrom and Ed Dayton are sensitive to all of this. They have said yes to God's claims upon their lives. They have bowed to His sovereignty as Lord of time. They also know Him as the Master of new things, the One who makes change possible in our life-styles—beginning with our most urgent needs.

My one word of advice to the reader is this: Plan to let this book change your ways. Between its covers is an uncommon amount of common sense. To the hurried and disorganized, it has words of peace and order. To the discouraged and disheartened, it offers keys of hope and expectation. To the apathetic and complacent, it presents prods to endeavor and achievement.

The book is winsomely written. Its phrases and illustrations point us in the directions we need to follow for Christian maturity.

Its instructions are practically implemented. Each theoretical point is made concrete by specific suggestions for carrying it out. We are never left to scratch our heads over the authors' meaning. Instead we are told just how to apply their points in our daily routines. The exercises and charts are easy to follow and will help nail each main idea in the reader's memory.

And this book has been personally demonstrated in the lives of the authors. Though they spend some time consulting with churches, businesses and Christian agencies worldwide, they spend more time supervising the highly efficient and carefully disciplined organizations of which they are part. They do not enjoy the consultant's luxury of learning at the other person's expense. They have practiced what they preach with extraordinary effectiveness. Above all, they have modeled that blend of spiritual and practical discipleship which is the essence of this book.

Wise persons, both ancient and modern, know the importance of planning carefully and using time frugally. They also know that God has plans beyond ours, plans that sometimes change ours. Ted Engstrom and Ed Dayton believe in God's sovereign will. They have heard clearly the other word of

Israel's wise men: "A man's mind plans his way, but the Lord directs his steps" (Prov. 16:9, *RSV*).

So we do our best, our most consecrated planning, and we leave all kinds of room for God's surprises. They must be part of our plan.

Our discipline and God's freedom conspire to bring excitement to every day and fruitfulness in due season. That combination—what we plan and what God does beyond our plans—is the core of our strategy for Christian living.

This book, as well as any that I know, points the way. Plan to let it change your life.

David A. Hubbard

Dr. David A. Hubbard, President
Fuller Theological Seminary
Pasadena, California

TO THOSE WHO HELPED

The many footnotes in the book attest to the fact that we have attempted to draw widely from the experience of other professionals. We continue to be learners and are grateful for how much the experience and careful research of others have contributed to us.

There are some men and women to whom we owe a special word of thanks. Dr. Gerald Foster, Professor of Public Administration at Denver University, gave us a sabbatical year in evaluating the effectiveness of the Managing Your Time Seminars and the concepts that are in this book. Dr. James Schmook has given us a valuable critique of the seminar and has added to us during those times when he has been a co-teacher.

Mrs. Carol Kocherhans has been both skilled and patient as we have continuously revised not only our seminar notes, but draft after draft of this manuscript.

We are grateful to them all.

HOW TO USE THIS BOOK

This book has been designed to give you a strategy, a strategy for Christian living. This strategy is very simply stated:

- Decide what it is God wants you to do and be—SET GOALS.
- Discover which goals are more important—ESTABLISH PRIORITIES.
- Analyze the best way to reach your goals—DO YOUR PLANNING.
- Start working toward your goals according to your plans—START LIVING.
- Use what you have learned to set new goals.

Strategies so simply stated are not always so easily understood. So we have arranged this book to help you move easily, first through understanding the details of an effective Christian life, and then on to seeing a total approach to living.

The concept is pictured by a circle of living: *goals, priorities, planning, living.* We want you to be able to use this simple diagram as a basis for all that you do, all of life.

We have ended each chapter with steps you can take

personally to make sure that you both understand and can make practical use of the ideas we are presenting. Wherever possible we have also suggested things you can do with your spouse or with your family. After all, for most of us, living life is a family affair.

We have given you a number of worksheet examples which are simple enough for you to copy and use yourself.

We have put notes at the end of chapters in the hope that if you want to dig further in a particular subject, you will have the resources to do so.

Different ways you can read this book are:

- You can read it straight through and get the overall concepts.
- You can pause at the end of each chapter and attempt some of the exercises.
- You can put it aside while you attempt to practice some of the suggested ideas in your everyday living.
- You can move directly to Part V and pick out areas that will work for you right now, even before you understand the total concept.

What we propose is not a rigid system. It will easily adapt itself to the high school student as well as the senior citizen, to the housewife as well as to the executive. Different approaches work for different people. Select those ideas which will be of most benefit to you.

Read this book with a pen or a pencil. Mark it up. Note the key ideas. Make notes in the margin. List those pages that are important to you.

And through it all, keep referring back to that simple diagram: GOALS, PRIORITIES, PLANNING, LIVING. This is the key around which the entire book is designed.

We know of hundreds of men and women who have discovered that the principles given in this book really work. We know they can work for you, too!

PART I THE STRATEGY

1 You Need a Strategy for Living
2 How We Discovered the Strategy

CHAPTER 1

YOU NEED A STRATEGY FOR LIVING

The telephone keeps ringing. Requests for another committee meeting, another involvement, another social engagement pile up. You measure the days that you have spent with your children, the times when you have been able to quietly contemplate your loved one's familiar face, and you count them all too few.

Some people tell you, "Jesus is the answer." But perhaps you are not even sure what the questions are. You believe that in the Bible you find the only infallible rule of faith and practice for your life, but the Bible doesn't always seem to be tailored for these complex, hectic days.

You wonder, then, is the problem really a question of *faith?* After all, you believe very sincerely in all of the things that the Bible teaches. But it doesn't seem to "work." Have you ever felt like that?

It happens in different ways to different people. For some it is an overwhelming sense of failure that suddenly engulfs them. For others it is a grueling sort of thing, a kind of a nagging that everything is not just right, a dissatisfaction with this life called Christian.

In our moments of more heightened awareness, we may recognize that the world *is* growing more complex. There is a closing inwardness to life. Perhaps it is just a function of growing old. But age is a relative thing, and for some it comes all too young.

What to do?

We have all heard what the *problem* is: communication overload. Too many messages from too many sources. Too many demands on our time. Too many problems to solve. The job at the office seems to get tougher. Vacations seem to come at greater intervals. Making ends meet at home gets harder. The deep sense of fellowship that you felt with a kindred few ten years ago has now been replaced by a multitude of superficial relationships.

You feel that you are just not measuring up. There are too many problems. Perhaps the confidence you began with a few years back, that confidence that some day you really would make it, has been replaced by a growing sense of despair.

Where are you going?

Where have you *been?* Perhaps another seminar, another good book. Perhaps you will meet a "significant other" one day who has just the right answer. Perhaps. But that is really not the answer, is it?

You see yourself on some uphill climb, on some ladder of life that seems to disappear in the clouds above. One day you will have children. One day they will be through school. One day there will be a better job. One day the children will be married. One day you will have more freedom to travel. One day you will be retired. And then, of course, one day you will die.

But What of Life?

Where did life go? Were those promises of a victorious Christian life just hollow words? Were they meant for another day, another time?

We think not. We don't think there are any *easy* answers. Life *is* a struggle. And that's all right. But there *is* an answer. There *is* a way to become a more effective person. And it is expressed in the answers to the same biblical questions we have always asked: What should we do? What should we be?

Paul gives us an answer: "Live life . . . with a due sense of responsibility, not as men [and women] who do not know the meaning and purpose of life but as *those who do*. Make the best use of your time, despite all the difficulties of these days" (Eph. 5:15,16, *Phillips*).

Each one of us has been given responsibility for himself. Each one of us is an individual before God. Each one of us has all the gifts that God meant us to have. In the many different roles that we play, in the many different situations of life that we face, under the many demands that are placed upon us, we are faced with ourselves, managing our lives, finding a strategy to live by.

Not a Formula but a Strategy

What we offer in the pages that follow is no simple formula. We do not promise that you will become happy, wealthy or "successful," but we do believe that what you will find here is an approach to the total Christian life-style that will make you a more effective and God-honoring person.

It is a strategy for life, a strategy for Christian living. Surprisingly simple and effective, it can be stated in one sentence: *Set your goals, establish your priorities, work out plans to reach those goals, and then measure life and your days against those goals.*

It looks simple. It *is* simple. And the reason it is so simple is that this is the way most of us live.

21

Each of us goes through life responding to his or her *goals*. We may not call them "goals," but that is what they are. How we are living at any moment is determined by the goal toward which we are moving. If our goals are clear and good, chances are we will be living well. But if our goals are poor or muddled, chances are that life will feel poor and muddled.

What we need then are *priorities*. We need to know that we are working on the best and most important goals.

Goals are what motivate us toward the future; but goals without plans are like a ship with a destination, but without a rudder. You may be moving, but you will have very little control over your direction. Good goals deserve good *planning*.

When we have chosen high, God-honoring goals, and when we have prayerfully done our planning, we have taken the first steps toward a strategy for Christian *living*.

It's a Process

But life is a process. We learn as we live. The Holy Spirit is continually teaching us new things. God uses our everyday experiences to help us discover better goals and more effective ways of reaching them. We need to see that a strategy for Christian living is a *process*.

So a *strategy* for Christian living is a circle: Goals need priorities; prioritized goals require planning; good planning helps us to live effective lives; effective living will help us set new and better goals.

That's the strategy: goals, priorities, planning, living.

Remember it! Live it! Make it part of everything you do. It is a strategy to give you freedom. It is a strategy to give you life.

THE STRATEGY

- HOW WE LIVE OUR LIFE IS
  DETERMINED BY OUR **GOALS**

- WHAT GOALS WE CHOOSE ARE
  DETERMINED BY OUR **PRIORITIES**

- WHETHER WE REACH OUR GOALS IS
  DETERMINED BY OUR **PLANNING**

- A STRATEGY FOR **LIVING**
  NEEDS GOOD GOALS
  CHRISTIAN PRIORITIES
  EFFECTIVE PLANS

- IT IS IN THE LIVING THAT WE FIND
  BETTER GOALS
  HIGHER PRIORITIES
  MORE EFFECTIVE PLANS

- THE STRATEGY IS A **PROCESS**
  GOALS—PRIORITIES—
  PLANNING—LIVING

TRY IT! IT WORKS!

CHAPTER 2

HOW WE DISCOVERED
THE STRATEGY

It all got started when we were asked by Tom Skinner, one of America's outstanding black Christian leaders, to put together a management training seminar for other black leaders. Along with Alex MacKenzie, who co-authored the book *Managing Your Time,*[1] we spent three and a half exciting days with 40 black leaders from the East Coast. During those three and a half days, many of their lives were transformed, and so were ours. In the midst of 40 loving, learning and enthusiastic brothers in Christ, we saw the power of management principles produce change in individuals. When applied the principles wrought changes of double benefit. Men and women were changed both in their on-the-job performance and in their basic life-style.

We were encouraged to accept other invitations to share what we had learned about management and managing a

Christian enterprise. Always we were faced with the question of how fundamental management principles could be applied to everyday Christian living. For it was our growing conviction that if what we did at our work or our business, if the way we earned a living, was something completely different than what we did in the rest of our life, we were not really living lives that were Christian. Life *had* to be a whole.

What had begun as responses to informal invitations slowly developed into a well-honed two-day seminar. We call them Managing Your Time seminars, but time is *life.* We became convinced that there was no sense in training Christian leaders to set goals and make plans for their Christian work if they were not first able to do this in their personal lives. So the first day of the seminar was spent covering much of the material that we have included in this book.

From the beginning the response was enthusiastic. At the end of each seminar we asked for an evaluation of effectiveness. Results were almost uniformly positive. In addition, we received many unsolicited letters thanking us for what had been learned. But the question was: Would it work in the long run? Were we just putting on an entertaining seminar, or was it really changing lives?

Seven years have passed. Now we have had opportunity to go back and visit the same pastors and lay leaders again. The results have been both challenging and rewarding. Our files are full of testimonials that the basic principles *do* work. Many organizations have adapted the material for their own use.

But we are challenged by the fact that we are unable to schedule one-quarter of the seminars that we would like to. So here they are in this book for your use. Learn them. Share them with others. Teach them. Use this book as a textbook to help others understand that there is a fundamental approach to effective living.

We have already outlined the strategy in Chapter 1. It is built around a process, with four key words: Goals, Priorities,

26

Planning, Living. And that is how the next major sections of this book are organized:

Part II—Goals (Chapters 3-6)
Part III—Priorities (Chapters 7-9)
Part IV—Planning (Chapters 10,11)
Part V—Living (Chapters 12,13)

A final section (Part VI) is called "Closing the Circle" and includes Chapters 14-18. This section helps you integrate the entire strategy for all of life and also gives you valuable tips on time management.

Participants at our Managing Your Time seminars receive an unusual graduation certificate. It is a gold-plated ruler inscribed with three simple but crucial words: GOALS—PRIORITIES—PLANNING. As you read the rest of this book, we hope that you will discover that these three words will be *your* golden rule for the very important business of LIVING effectively.

Footnote

1. Ted W. Engstrom and Alex MacKenzie, *Managing Your Time* (Grand Rapids: Zondervan, 1967). An overall approach to managing a Christian enterprise.

PART II GOALS

3 Goals Have Power to Change You
4 You Need Goals to Live By
5 Goals Give Purpose to Your Life
6 Put Your Goals to Work

CHAPTER 3

GOALS HAVE POWER TO CHANGE YOU

The world is continually offering us choices. The futurists of our day tell us that we are suffering from over-choice. There are just too many decisions to make. We become confused.

"What model of car shall I buy? What options should it have? Would it be better to buy a used car or a new one?"

"What dress should I buy? Will the style change?"

"Where should my children go to school?"

"Where should we live?"

"Is this the right job for me?"

"Should I accept this committee assignment, or would I be better off teaching a Sunday School class?"

"Where shall we eat dinner tonight?"

"What suit shall I wear tomorrow?"

"Shall we redecorate the living room?"

All of this is the result of living in an affluent Western society.

The farmer scratching out a living in a village in India faces no such problems. His goal is very clear. He wants to survive. And that clear goal keeps him pushing on.

He wakes up each morning knowing exactly what he has to do toward that goal. Passersby may offer interruptions. His children may be looking for attention. There may be a big political rally in the next village. But that Indian farmer will not be distracted. His goal is set, his priorities are clear, and his plans are made.

Goals Are Motivators

Goals are one of the most powerful motivating forces known to man. In a delightful little book, psychiatrist Dr. Ari Kiev of Cornell Medical Center states, "With goals people can overcome confusion and conflict over incompatible values, contradictory desires and frustrated relationships with friends and relatives, all of which often result from the absence of rational life strategies.

"Observing the lives of people who have mastered adversity, I have repeatedly noted that they have established goals and, irrespective of obstacles, sought with all their effort to achieve them. From the moment they've fixed an objective in their mind and decide to concentrate all their energies on a specific goal, they begin to surmount the most difficult odds."[1]

We have all seen this, haven't we? Billy Graham has become the world's leading evangelist because he has focused on what it was he wanted to do and moved toward that goal with God-given determination. William Carey, "the father of modern missions," set his mind and heart on carrying the gospel to India. His refusal to be turned aside by circumstances or individuals launched a missionary enterprise that is still gaining momentum today.

We All Have Goals

In one sense, we all have goals. We may not be aware of

them, but they are there. God has placed in us all basic drives which motivate us toward certain types of goals. The psychologist, Abraham Maslow, described these motivators as a "hierarchy of needs,"[2] (Fig. A).

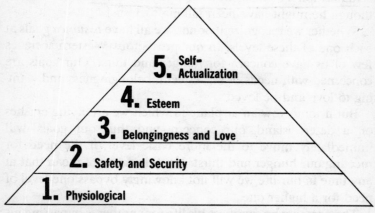

MASLOW'S HIERARCHY OF NEEDS

Figure A

At the very foundation of our being are *physiological* needs. We must have food and water to merely stay alive. When we are dying of thirst, our entire attention is focused on one goal: Get water!

At a higher level, there are needs for *safety* and *security*. When we are alone on a deserted city street at midnight, our primary goal is to arrive home safely.

Once these needs are met we can then turn our thoughts to *loving* and *being loved* and feeling as though we are a part of the group. We set goals to deepen friendships or to care for our children.

One step higher on the scale is *esteem,* the need for self-respect, a feeling of self-worth. To have high self-esteem is to feel good about being you.[3]

At the top of Maslow's hierarchy is the need for what he calls *self-actualization*. By self-actualization Maslow means we should become so free we are no longer concerned with self. Maslow visualizes the self-actualized person finding his self-actualization in giving himself away to others. It sounds as though he might have been talking to Jesus!

Whether we recognize it or not, we all have *assumed* goals at each one of these levels. In our prosperous Western societies few of us have concern for hunger and thirst. Our goals are concerned with needs of self-esteem, belongingness and wanting to love and be loved.

But if tomorrow an airplane in which we are flying crashes on a desert island, our concern—and thus our goals—will immediately move to the more basic level of the need for meeting our hunger and thirst. Yet this does not mean that at any time in our life we will not knowingly bypass one level of need for a higher one.

The person who sacrifices his life for another is bypassing his needs for safety to meet a higher need. How well we understand Jesus' cry to His Father, "If it is possible, let this cup be taken away from me" (Matt. 26:39, *TLB*). How grateful we are that He was willing to give up the goal of survival for a higher goal.

Goals, then, are primary motivators for life. If we understand our goals, we will better understand our life. *If we change our goals, we change our life.*

Understand Where You Fit

For the Christian the secret of managing your life is to prayerfully define what kind of a life you believe God wants you to lead, to attempt *to understand where you fit in His strategy.* A way to do this is to set specific goals for things that you want to happen in your life in the days ahead. Over and over we have discovered that the person who has clear, strong goals is the person who lives the most effective life.

What is it you want to do with your life? How will the world be different because you have been here? What are your hopes and dreams for your family, for your church, for those with whom you work?

What should you be doing five years from now? What should you be doing next year, next week? The answers to each one of these questions can be stated as a goal, but they need to be fitted together into a mosaic that is a design for *your* life.

"Live life, then, with a due sense of responsibility, not as men [and women] who do not know the meaning and purpose of life but as *those who do*" (Eph. 5:15,16, *Phillips*).

Summing Up

Where we are going and what we want to do is best expressed in terms of goals. Goals can be stated for all areas of our lives. They need to be integrated together in a way which gives us a total picture of our life.

Something for You to Do

Complete the following sentences:

1. My greatest goal in life is to_____ .
2. Five years from now I would like to have_____ .
3. By the end of this year I hope that I will have_____ .
4. This week I hope to_____ .

Footnotes

1. Ari Kiev, *A Strategy for Daily Living* (New York: Free Press, 1973), p. 3.
2. Abraham H. Maslow, *Motivation and Personality* (New York: Harper and Row, 1954). Keith Miller has handled Maslow's concept well in his book, *The Becomers* (Waco, TX: Word, 1973).
3. For more about self-esteem, see Dorothy Corkille Briggs' *Your Child's Self-Esteem* (Garden City, NY: Doubleday and Co., 1970).

CHAPTER 4

YOU NEED GOALS
TO LIVE BY

A goal is a statement about how we hope things are going to be at some time in the future. It is a statement of *faith.*

Any statement about tomorrow is a statement of faith. This is an important concept. Don't miss it. As the writer in Hebrews said, "Faith is the substance of things hoped for" (Heb. 11:1).

Goals have the power to lift our eyes from the mud below toward the sky above. They are statements about what could be, what should be, what *can* be.

Notice that goals are not statements about what *will* be. That is in God's hands.

Goals for living a Christian life are our response to God. But we *can* go further. Goals are statements about what we believe we need to *do* as well as what we need to *be.*

Goals Help Us Psychologically

At a psychological level, goals help us answer the questions,

"Who am I? Where have I been? Where am I going? What do I do next?"

Most of us know those feelings of uncertainty. We suddenly realize that things just are not clear. We need to believe that we have control of things, that all of the future is not just one big unknown.

Goals can help. They are like signposts along the road, which help us keep a sense of direction. They tell us how far we have been and how far we have yet to go. Goal statements about different areas of our life help us to see discrepancies in some of the things that we are doing and help us to live a more integrated life.

Goals give us the ability to take the emphasis off the negative—problems of the present—and focus our thinking on the positive—future possibilities. What a good feeling it is to know that we have already passed a goal! And the knowledge of other goals yet lying before us gives us the motivation to move forward (Fig. A).

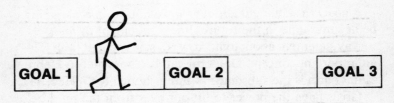

Figure A

How easy it is to become depressed over the mess that you are in. You are feeling "down," really blue. You are not even sure why. But then you decide to *do* something about it. You set a goal to accomplish something, say, by tomorrow. Immediately your thoughts are taken away from the now.

How often have you heard someone say something like, "My, I feel better now that I have made a decision to *do* something!"?

Goals Help Us Physically

If we haven't set any goals, if we haven't established some milestones along the path, then we won't know where we are. But when we divide up the journey into specific goals, we can tell where we've been and where we're going.

You have to get the house ready for a party. There are a thousand things to do, it seems. Break it down into sub-goals, let's say to clean one room at a time. Five rooms to clean? Two done? We are on our way, aren't we?

At a physical level, goals help us to sort out the demands on our time. If we know what we *intend* to do, what we believe that we should do, then it is much easier for us to recognize when our time or attention is being diverted from that which we believe God would have us to do.

Take a look at your calendar. Is it filled up with all kinds of appointments which other people have asked you to make? How many of those dates in your appointment book were initiated by you? How many were just responses to what someone asked you to do? Those dates on the calendar are really your plan for living the next few weeks. *Are they God-approved.*

When the calendar includes goals for what we want to accomplish, things that relate to our life, then we are less harried, less pushed. For we are doing the things we believe *God wants* us to do, rather than things that other people think we should do. We will have more to say about this in Chapter 14 as we discuss living a strategic life.

The everyday nitty-gritty of the physical level immediately relates to family life, doesn't it? Here we need to share our goals so we can agree on common ones. For example, people tell us how disappointed they were with their family vacation. It just didn't seem to please anyone. On closer examination, they often discover that they had not adequately shared their individual expectations of the purpose (goals) of their vacation.

Dad may have thought that he was going to go fishing. He could almost smell the fish frying over an open campfire.

Mother may have expected they were going to the lake to give her a break from household chores. How nice to lie in bed in the morning knowing there was no breakfast to prepare! Junior may have thought of the lake as a place to learn to water ski. He had been saving money for weeks for this.

Dad never did understand why Mother wasn't overjoyed with sleeping in a tent. And Junior couldn't get all excited about the small motor on the rowboat they had rented. The lack of shared goals led to disappointment for them all.

Goals Help Us Socially

At a social level, goals help us to express our responsibility to all men. And we *do* have a responsibility. As James puts it, "The man who makes no allowances for others will find none made for him. It is still true that 'mercy smiles in the face of judgment' " (Jas. 2:13, *Phillips*). We are born into a world of persons. We are born into a world in which we have responsibility to all men and all women. No man is an island! If we make no statements (set no goals) about our response to world need and responsibility, then we are left with a sense of uneasiness or guilt about what we should do. We cannot do everything. We can set specific goals to do something. How do you help a billion starving people?

One at a time![1]

The need for shared goals becomes more important every day. We are living in a technological society that is becoming more and more splintered. Instead of the homogenous melting pot we hoped for, we find an ever-growing number of minorities. If we maintain a stance of "rugged individualism," we will increasingly discover, to use Philip Slater's phrase, we are in pursuit of loneliness.[2] That is not only a weary business, it completely ignores the biblical understanding that we are part of one another (see 1 Cor. 12). God meets us individually, one by one. But He immediately makes us part of a body.

When we have a shared goal to accomplish something or to

do something together with someone else, we discover that this can bring us a sense of oneness and a sense of belonging. We build strong relationships with others more rapidly when we are working on a common task than when we just set out to establish a relationship for its own sake.

We find our friends among those with whom we work, whether it be at the office or at the church. The reasons are not difficult to understand. Since we share a common motivation to accomplish something, we also share a sense of common destiny. We see one another as people who have the same desire, the same needs, people who are "like us." We are naturally attracted to people who share common goals with us. The contrary is also true. We tend to move away from people whose goals seem different than our own.[3]

Goals Help Us Spiritually

At a spiritual level, we can see three strong reasons for setting goals. First, goals lie in the future. Christians should be people who live in the present *and* in the future.

Paul sums it up when he says, "Forgetting what is behind me, and reaching out for that which lies ahead, I press towards the goal to win the prize which is God's call to the life above, in Christ Jesus" (Phil. 3:13,14, *NEB*).

Christianity rejects the view of human personality as being fixed at a very early age.[4] Christians should be growing and developing people. In one sense, they should be the most secure of all people. Their past is forgiven and their future is secure! Each day brings with it potential for a new beginning.

If you woke up this morning and confessed your failures and sins to the Lord, He sees you as a new person. The past with all of its failures is rolled up like a rug behind you. God assures you that He has put those failures completely out of His sight. "As far as the east is from the west, so far hath he removed our transgressions from us" (Ps. 103:12).

What a fantastic idea! God has forgotten what lies behind, so you can forget it, too. You can be confident in the belief that as you seek to find His will for your life, He will take part in making you what you should be. Today *is* the first day of the rest of your life!

The second dimension of our spiritual need for goals is wrapped up in the biblical imperative "You, therefore, must be perfect [complete], as your heavenly Father is perfect" (Matt. 5:48, *RSV*). We are given the assurance that there *is* a standard. We are not building our lives on shifting sand.

God has placed us in a world where good is good. What is perfect is perfect. On the other hand, the tension of such a statement is immediately apparent. "It is the straightedge of the Law that shows us how crooked we are" (Rom. 3:20, *Phillips*).

God says, "You must be perfect!"

And inside we respond, "Oh, but I'm not perfect, and I know it!"

So all we can do is fall back on God's mercy, thanking Him for the fact that He does forgive us when we fail, yet also rejoicing in the fact that we can expect to find standards against which we can set high goals. These goals become our statements of faith, statements that we believe there is an ultimate standard and that it is our intention to set goals to reach it.

A third spiritual need for goals is to give us a way to respond to our understanding of God's plan for our lives. Too often we stop at Ephesians 2:9 and forget that we are born afresh in Christ, and born "to do those good deeds which God planned for us to do" (Eph. 2:10, *Phillips*).

Now here is a paradox. We can't understand how it is possible that we have freedom and yet at the same time, God has "plans" for us. About the best we can do with that intellectually is to recognize that when we live our lives accepting that paradox, *it works.*

We need faith that in the midst of our freedom, God has good things He wants us to do and to be. As we in faith set goals for the future, we demonstrate our trust in the fact that God is not playing games with us. He always desires only our good.[5]

In all of this the Christian has a particular advantage, for the Christian has a straight-line view of history. He sees all of life moving purposefully toward a culmination. We are not like the Hindu who can look forward only to his next reincarnation. We have an eternal hope. We believe that there is an ultimate explanation to all of the mystery of life.

We may not understand exactly how what we are doing is related to what all the other members of the Body of Christ are doing. We may not know how our goals fit everyone else's goals. But even as we see through a glass darkly, we can rest in the confidence that God is taking all of the events of our life and using them for His glory.

Doing vs. Being

As Christians the Bible calls us to be more concerned with what we are than what we accomplish. Interestingly, however, what we are in an ethical sense is always expressed in terms of relationships. The righteous, the loving, the kind, the forbearing, the good—these are all statements about relationships.

Of course, there is an inner life. One can sin in one's heart. But inner sins are actually a failure in our relationship to the Person of God.

Very seldom are we able to state a measurable and accomplishable goal for those things that we should *be*. Here again is the paradox: what we *are* is measured by what we *do*. When we attempt to write goals about what we should be, we quickly recognize that they can only be expressed in terms of what we should do.[6]

Why Are Some People Afraid of Goals?

Probably the greatest fear we have of setting goals is the fear of failure. Somehow we feel that if we have made a statement about something we are going to do or something we are going to accomplish, if we don't do it or accomplish it, we will have

43

become a lesser person. Others will not regard us as highly as they did before. There is some truth in this. If we continually "fail," people will conclude that we are a "failure." People respond to this fear in some interesting ways. Some people set their goals so high they are always impossible to meet. "Let's shoot to have 500 people at church next week!" The goal is so high that everyone understands that it won't be met. Others consistently set their goals low enough so that they're always sure of success. "Suppose we plan on having 75 people here next week."

There is a way out of this tension. The most effective people are those who set their goals just beyond what they can reasonably expect of themselves. "They set moderately difficult, but potentially achievable goals. In biology, this is known as the *overload principle*. In weight lifting, for example, strength cannot be increased by tasks that are performed easily or that cannot be performed without stress to the organism. Strength can be increased by lifting weights that are difficult, but realistic enough to stretch the muscles."[7]

A second reason why people are afraid to set goals is they are concerned that they may be "doing the work of the Holy Spirit." They fear that to make any statement about the future is presumptuous. "After all, our times are in God's hands, aren't they? Doesn't James 4:13 tell us not to say we are going to do this or that tomorrow?" No, James tells us to recognize that while we are pursuing our plans there is always the dimension, "if God wills."

For the Christian, the first antidote for this fear is to recognize that God *is* sovereign. The second is to understand that goals are statements of faith, statements about what we believe God wants us to do or to be. The reason the Christian can pursue the goal of excellence is because his failure to achieve is not a reflection on *his person*. That is established. We are not measured in God's sight by our successes or our failures.

Summing Up

Goals are important to us psychologically, physically, socially and spiritually. For the Christian who believes that the Holy Spirit gives him the power to become different than he is, goals are particularly important. They are personal statements of faith.

Some people are afraid to set goals for fear that they may fail. Others are afraid to set goals because they feel that they are doing the work of the Holy Spirit. The first is the failure to trust God to do the work. The second is the failure to realize that God expects us to be about His business.

Something for You to Do

Think of goals that you have set for yourself during the past six months. Which of these did you achieve? Which did you not achieve? Would things have gone better if you had not set any goals but just let things happen? Why?

Footnotes

1. An excellent statement about what the individual can do is Stanley Mooneyham's *What Do You Say to a Hungry World?* (Waco, TX: Word, 1975).
2. See Philip E. Slater's *Pursuit of Happiness* (Boston: Beacon Press, 1971).
3. We ignore this principle to our peril. One of the reasons that many church committees function so poorly is that they have been given a function to perform with no idea of the common goal the function serves.
4. For further reading in the area of personality theory, see Gordon Allport's *Pattern and Growth in Personality* (New York: Holt, Rinehart and Winston, 1961). See also Allport's *Becoming: Basic Considerations for a Psychology of Personality* (New Haven: Yale University Press, 1955).
5. You will find paradoxes and tension like this throughout the rest of the book. Part of living in faith is to live in paradox, for the Bible calls us to act on *all* of God's commands. For a good discussion of some of these paradoxes and how to handle them, see Virginia Mollenkott's *In Search of Balance* (Waco, TX: Word, 1959) and Gerald Kennedy's *The Lion and the Lamb* (Nashville: Abingdon Press, 1950).
6. For a recent discussion on how our beliefs should issue forth in ethics, read Bernard L. Ramm's *The Right, the Good, and the Happy* (Waco, TX: Word, 1971).
7. Paul Hersey and Kenneth H. Blanchard, *Management of Organization Behavior* (Englewood Cliffs, NJ: Prentice-Hall, 1969), p. 35.

CHAPTER 5

GOALS GIVE PURPOSE
TO YOUR LIFE

What about setting goals for life? How do we go about it? Where do we begin? We begin by first coming to terms with a few words.

Words are very important to Christians. Such words as *sanctification, justification* and *salvation* are words that are full of meaning and power for us.

We Christians particularly tend to state what we believe in terms, or propositions, which are carefully framed and worded. If you have ever taken part in the framing of a statement of faith for a new organization, you know what we mean.

At a personal level, when we do a word study in the Bible, we become particularly concerned with shades and nuances and meanings of words and phrases. And yet when it comes to *action,* too often we are content to leave words like "purposes" and "goals" in some foggy undefined area. We talk about the grand purpose we have "to give glory to God," "to go into all the world," "to lead God-honoring lives." Good. These are words and phrases which we need in our everyday language as Christians. But they can so easily become passwords by which we identify one another, rather than statements of what we really intend to do. At a missionary meeting we attended we heard that the purpose of one group was "to bring all of Japan to the feet of Christ." What does that mean? It's verbal fog.

Get Out of the Fog

Verbal fog can completely incapacitate us. We may desire to be a God-honoring father or mother. We may pray earnestly that God will make us such a parent. We may feel all kinds of love toward our children and have grand ideals for them. We may earnestly quote, "Train up a child in the way he should go: and when he is old, he will not depart from it" (Prov. 22:6). But the question is: What are we going to *do?* How does a God-honoring father *act?* What does one do to train up a child in the way he should go? How can we *know* whether what we did was effective or ineffective if we really did not decide what we *intended* to do?

A Goal Is a Measurable Purpose

When a baseball player stands up at the plate, his goal is very clear and measurable. His goal is not to be a "good ballplayer." At that moment in time his goal is to get a base hit.

His goal is *measurable.* It is *accomplishable.* He will know when he has done it or failed to do it. And he is not afraid of failure. He knows that even the best ballplayer fails to get a hit more than six out of every ten times at bat.

A parent needs to have the same kind of measurable goals. "In order to be a better father, I intend to spend four hours playing ball with my son every Saturday morning." We have no way of *being sure* that spending those four hours will really produce a more effective father. But we do have a clear statement of intentions.

Purposes vs. Goals

We need to start with *purposes* in our lives. We need great visions, grand dreams, great faith. But God expects us to take our faith a step further and set goals—statements about the future that are measurable and accomplishable.

A *purpose,* then, is an aim or direction, something which we want to achieve, but something which is not necessarily measurable.

A *goal,* on the other hand, is a future event which we believe is both accomplishable and measurable. Measurable in terms of what is to be done and how long it takes to do it.

To be a great mountain climber is "a purpose." To climb Pike's Peak during the month of January is "a goal." To purchase all the climbing gear necessary to climb Pike's Peak by December may or may not be a goal depending upon whether "all the climbing gear necessary" is well established. It may be better to have said, "Purchase climbing shoes, backpack and a canteen by December."

To really understand God's Word is a purpose. To take specific training in leading neighborhood Bible studies by next June is a goal. To hold one neighborhood Bible study each week for ten weeks is a goal.

How to Write Good Goals

One way to get this distinction in perspective is to attempt to write a few goals and notice the difference between goals and purposes. But before you try, look at the characteristics of well-written goals and poorly written goals in Figure A.

If you find that you have difficulty in writing a goal for a particular purpose, try breaking the goal down into its various parts—or sub-goals—and writing goals for each of these. In this way you will still get what you want—a definable, measurable, accomplishable goal.

To go back to the illustration of trying to be an effective father, we may find that in order to recognize our purpose of being an effective father, we have to list a number of goals. These might be: (1) to spend four hours each Saturday morning

WELL WRITTEN GOALS	POORLY WRITTEN GOALS
Stated in terms of end results.	Stated in terms of process or activities.
Achievable in definite time.	Are never fully achievable: No specific target dates.
Definite as to what is expected.	Ambiguous as to what is expected.
Practical and feasible.	Theoretical or idealistic.
Precisely stated in terms of quantities, where applicable.	Too brief and indefinite or too long and complex.
Limited to one important goal or statement.	Written with two or more goals per statement.

Figure A

playing ball with my son; (2) to make sure that at least 15 minutes of the discussion around the dinner table is centered on the activities of our children; (3) to have a weekly planning session to decide on what TV programs we will watch.

We could diagram it something like Figure B.

So we see that a purpose is the summation of a number of goals and sub-goals. There is no *one* specific goal that will meet the purpose; all make up the whole.

To use another illustration, goals are the bricks with which purposes are built. The goals come in all shapes and sizes and fit together to build the chief purposes of our lives. Individually, some goals may seem like small, even inconsequential things. But together our goals make us what we are and what we intend to be.[1]

Relating Goals to One Another

In the same way that all of our actions are entwined, so are our goals. There are big ones and little ones, some that should

PURPOSE
TO BE
AN EFFECTIVE FATHER

I NEED THESE GOALS

GOAL 1	GOAL 2	GOAL 3
Spend 4 hours with my son.	Center part of dinner table discussion on children.	Have weekly family TV planning session.

Figure B

happen very soon and some that are far away. Some goals are dependent upon others.

Let us use a golf game as an illustration. My long-range goal for the golf game is to have a lower total score than any of my opponents. However, my long-range goal is really the summation of a series of intermediate goals—my score for each hole. Each of these is made up of some immediate goals, such as the goal of sinking a 15-foot putt.

All of these goals are not only related in time, but they are also dependent upon one another. I can't move on to reaching

51

a goal of completing the *second hole* until I have met my goal of completing the first hole. And so it goes.

"All right," you say, "I've got that. I can see how it would really be great if I had some clear idea of what I wanted to do and to be. Having measurable goals sounds good. But *how* do I do it?

We will discuss that in the next chapter.

Summing Up

Our conscious and subconscious goals have tremendous power to motivate us. Our perceived goals are statements of faith about the future. They are our perception of what we should be and can be. Since all of life is controlled by our goals, *deciding* what kind of goals we will have is the first step toward living life with a purpose.

We need to differentiate between immeasurable *purposes* and measurable *goals*. A failure to do so can leave us incapacitated in a verbal fog. We need to begin with purpose in our lives but also to describe these in terms of goals.

Something for You to Do Alone

In Figure C is a list of sixteen statements about the future. Which are purposes and which are goals?[2] After you have checked, turn the page upside down for the answers.

Footnotes

1. We realize when we talk about goals that there is a wide variety of terminology. What we call a *purpose* some people might call a goal, a mission or an objective. What we call a *goal* others may call an objective, a milestone, a step or even a standard. But let's not get boxed in by definitions. Accept our terminology for the purposes of this book and then use whatever words for these terms are appropriate in your own setting.
2. For a delightful, compact discussion on the difference between purposes and goals, we recommend Robert Mager's *Goal Analysis* (Belmont, CA: Fearon Pub., 1972). Ed Dayton's *God's Purpose/Man's Plans* (Monrovia, CA: MARC, 1972) will also be useful here.

WHICH IS A PURPOSE—WHICH IS A GOAL?

THINGS I WANT TO DO OR BE	PURPOSE	GOAL
1. Have dinner with my family more often		
2. Read one book per week		
3. Work on fewer committees		
4. Spend 15 minutes in prayer each day		
5. Read the Bible more often		
6. Attend Sunday school and church every Sunday		
7. Learn more about personal counseling		
8. Learn to sail (or fly an airplane) by the end of summer		
9. Become a better tennis player		
10. Take a trip to the Holy Land (or Europe, Asia) next summer		
11. Be a more gracious person		
12. Make $10,000 a year by end of next year		
13. Think about buying a sports car		
14. Tithe a minimum of 10% of my income		
15. Live in a better home		
16. Move to Indianapolis by the end of next year		

The even numbered statements are goals.

Figure C

CHAPTER 6

PUT YOUR GOALS TO WORK

Goals are powerful motivators.

Goals are statements of faith about the future. They are our response to what we believe God wants us to be and do.

There is a difference between goals and purposes. Purposes are the grand aims toward which we move. Goals are the specifics of what we want to accomplish.

How do we go about discovering what we want to accomplish and setting goals? By following seven simple steps.

Seven Steps to Setting Goals

Step 1: Understand your purpose. What is it that you would like to do or to become? What is the general direction toward which you would like to move? Make a statement about that.

Step 2: Picture the situation. Imagine the situation not as it is now, but as you would like it to be. What does it look like? Who are you with? What are you doing? What are the circumstances?

Step 3: State some long-range goals. What measurable and accomplishable events would have to happen in order for that purpose to be realized?

Step 4: State your immediate goals. What are the things that you have to accomplish now if you are going to move toward your ultimate purpose?

Step 5: Act. Pick out one of the goals and start moving toward it. Remember that every long journey begins with the first step!

Step 6: Act as if . . . Act as if you have already reached your goal. If you are going to start working toward that first goal, you are going to have to start acting as if you had really reached it. How would this impact on all the other parts of your life? What would it say about your plans for your employer, your family, others? This may help you uncover some other goals that you need to consider.

Step 7: Keep praying. If you are going to live life with a purpose, then you need to keep seeking God's leading in all this. Yes, you have been praying through the whole planning process. But pray, as well, before you act. If you are expecting to live a life with God's purpose in mind, you had better be communicating with Him.

Notice in all of this that the steps to uncover goals move from the future *backward* to the present. This is the way we *plan.* When we go to *carry out* our plans we move in *the opposite direction.*

Tomorrow's Goals Impact on Today

Setting goals not only helps us to think about what we should do today, but it also forces us to anticipate the results of our present actions. So it has both long-range and short-range benefits.

Suppose, for example, that you as a husband are frustrated

by your inability to relate to your family when you come home from work. You arrive home tired, full of the problems of the day and anticipating the difficulties of tomorrow. Your mind is far away from your family, and your family knows it. You would like to relate to your children, but somehow it just doesn't seem to fit together.

Let us see, then, how the seven steps might work in a practical situation such as the one we have just outlined. Let's try this goal-setting process on a reasonably short-range basis. Suppose your purpose is "improving things at home on weekday evenings."

Step 1: Understand your purpose. Let's say that you would like to have evenings at home that have less tension and have a feeling of the family being more together.

Step 2: Picture the situation. What kind of a situation would you like to find when you are home from the office? Imagine what appears to you to be the ideal situation. As you consider such an ideal, how are you relating to your family? How are they relating to you? What are you saying to one another? What needs of your family can you meet? What are the needs that you have that they can meet?

Step 3: Set long-range goals. Set some specific goals for how things would be in your family, say six months from now. Perhaps you would like to have a weekly family sharing time. What would each member of the family have to do in order to help reach the goal of having a good time of sharing together?

Step 4: Set short-range goals. A pastor attending one of our seminars who has faced this same situation suggests that you set this short-range goal: As you drive home from the office, take time to focus in on the needs of each member of your family. Take time to think about the things they are going to be talking about and needing to hear from you. Get emotionally prepared for them.

While that may be an immediate, short-range goal from you, perhaps your wife needs the goal of planning and preparing the evening meal before you arrive home so she is free to be with you and the children. Perhaps the children's schedule needs to be changed around so they are more open and available. Or perhaps a much better solution would be for you to spend an hour alone with your wife when you first arrive home so you are really ready to enter into the children's activities after suppertime.

Step 5: Act. Pick one of these goals and go to work on it immediately. How about setting a goal to have considered each member's needs by the time you arrive home?

Step 6: Act as if . . . If you are going to change your thinking this evening, you should be acting that way through the day. Maybe this means that, as you head for your car, you have to start acting as if things are going to be all right at home that evening.

Step 7: Keep praying. Perhaps in the midst of this God will show you a better way.

The point is that by describing the situation as you would like to have it, you can take the steps now, make decisions now, about how you might arrive at that goal.

Most of us know that we need to "plan ahead." What we often fail to realize is that if we don't set specific goals, we really have nothing to plan ahead for.

But Is It Biblical?

Does the Bible spell out this approach to planning one's life? Not specifically. But there are innumerable illustrations from both the New and the Old Testaments of people who announced their intentions and then permitted God to be sovereign in their life. Illustrations from Paul's life are appropriate here. He told the Romans that after he had finished the work he was carrying out, it was his goal to visit them as he moved on to Spain (see Rom. 15:28). On the other hand, when he and his party attempted to go into Bithynia, they were prevented from moving in that direction by the Holy Spirit (see

Acts 16:7). Here we see the two sides of the situation. First, man proposing. Second, man being open to God's disposing.

Some Other Advantages of Goals

Goals that we share with others are ways of communicating where we are. By sharing goals with our associates and with our families, we *greatly strengthen communications.* Goal statements about different areas of our life help us to see discrepancies in some of the things that we are doing and help us to live a more integrated life.

It's a Process

Throughout this book, we will keep reemphasizing that what we are advocating here is a *process,* a way of *living life* in a way that will make it more pleasing to God. Perhaps the best way of thinking about this is to realize that this is a system of steering in the midst of the stream of life, not a way to build a dam. We are continually faced by the biblical paradox that our times are in His hands, even as we are responsible for our own lives.

There is more to living a purposeful life than just setting goals. We need to find ways to analyze our present commitments and situations and to see ourselves as whole persons.

We need to somehow find ways to live an integrated life.

We need to discover what is our Christian value system and then to find some ways to work this all through. We will discuss these things in the following chapters. The important thing is to understand that we have more control over our futures than most of us tend to believe. The key to living a purposeful life is to exercise our faith by setting specific goals for both the short-range and long-range future, and then using these goals as control points around which the rest of our life centers.[1,2]

Summing Up

Goals help us begin to live a purposeful life. There are seven simple steps to setting goals:

59

Step 1: Understand your purpose. What is it you want to have happen?

Step 2: Picture the situation. What would it be like?

Step 3: State some long-range goals. What steps would lead to this situation?

Step 4: State your immediate goals. What should you do now?

Step 5: Act. Do it!

Step 6: Act as if . . .

Step 7: Keep praying.

All of this is a process which can be applied to many different aspects of our life and eventually should be applied to our total life.

Something for You to Do

Think about a purpose that you would like to work on. Using the seven steps that we have suggested, decide what action you would have to take today to move toward that ultimate purpose.

Something to Do with Your Spouse

Decide together on a purpose that you would both like to work toward and then independently go through the seven steps. After you have done this, compare the goals that you and your spouse have listed. Where do they differ and why do they differ?

What would be needed to come up with a set of goals to which you both agree? There is a simple saying, "Good goals are *my* goals. Bad goals are your goals."

Make sure your goals are *our* goals!

Something to Do with Your Family

Lead your children through this same exercise. Pick something that they would like to do. Let them think of any way-out idea that comes up. After they have utilized all their fantasies to state the general situation they would like to be in someday, lead them backward from the future into the present. You will be surprised at what good goals they may suggest!

Footnotes

1. For some professional help in gaining an understanding of your likes and dislikes as well as your aptitudes, a number of tests, such as the Strong Vocational Aptitude Test are available through universities and through counseling centers. They are usually worth the investment.
2. For a charming narrative of one Christian's experience with attempting to develop a family strategy and set of family goals, read Don Osgood's *The Family and the Corporation Man* (New York: Harper and Row, 1975).

PART III PRIORITIES

GOALS

STRATEGY
FOR
LIVING

LIVING   PRIORITIES

PLANNING

7 How You Can Set Priorities
8 You Need to Make Decisions
9 Priorities and Christian Commitment

CHAPTER 7

HOW YOU CAN SET PRIORITIES

STRATEGY
FOR
LIVING

GOALS

PRIORITIES

LIVING

PLANNING

Goals, priorities and planning—these are the steps to move you toward living a purposeful life. We have talked about *goals,* what they are and what they are not. We suggested steps to coming up with some good goals. But what about *priorities?* How will you know which are the best goals? If your life has too many goals, what do you do?

In this chapter we give you some simple techniques that will help you to sort out your priorities. This will be groundwork for thinking about Christian priorities, which we will do later.

When We Need Priorities

We need to sort out our priorities when we have more goals than we know how to handle.

We need to sort out our priorities because the world keeps changing.

We need to sort out our priorities to decide what to do next.

You can have too many goals. If you sat down and made a list of all the goals it might be nice to have, the list would be endless. Get a new job? Take a trip to Hawaii? Spend Christmas with the family? Join the choir? Learn to play golf?

The world keeps changing. Things are never the way they should be. They very seldom are the way we plan them to be. Consequently, there will always be a need to re-juggle our priorities, to sort things out afresh.

And because things are never the way they should be, there is always a question of trade-offs. You will find this, for instance, in the life of your local church. Ideally every local church has a good balance between worship, evangelism, teaching and fellowship. Actually, the church that does have a good balance is a rarity.

Why?

Because there is a need for deciding what the priorities *are.* What comes first as most needful in your life just now and, consequently, in the life of your local church?

What to do next? In one sense all priority questions are "when" questions. We are trying to decide what to do next and what to do after that. The least important things we will never get around to.

Choose the Future

Over the entrance of the Archives Building in Washington, D.C., is the phrase "What is past is prologue." The past can have a fascination for us. Phrases like "We've always done it this way" or "We tried that and it didn't work" can be deadly in considering a new goal.

Too often we have become enmeshed in pursuing a goal that was very appropriate five, ten or twenty years ago, but which is meaningless today.[1]

So our first question might be: *Is this just a goal out of the past? Does it really have to do with the future?*

Priority Questions

Following are some other questions you can ask about your goals which will help you sort out your priorities:

How urgent is it? When must it be done? Right now? Today? Soon? Someday?

General Eisenhower is quoted as saying, "The urgent is seldom important, and the important is seldom urgent." Too often life is controlled by the "tyranny of the urgent." We put aside higher and more worthy goals to put out fires.

The trouble is, many of us *enjoy* putting out fires. "Fire fighting" can become a major purpose in our lives. It distracts us from some of the other difficulties that we need to face further along the road. And it gives us a wonderful excuse to move along with the tide of circumstances.

We have all met fire fighters, haven't we? They have a breathless urgency about them. There is a large problem out there that only *they* can handle.

There are probably fire fighters in your church, your shop, your office, your family. Maybe *you* are one!

How important is it? Very important? Quite important? Somewhat important? Not so important?

This question of importance will force us back to our reasons for setting the goal in the first place. What is the *why* of it?

Not everything we do can be important. But some things should be. There are great chunks of life which are routine and somewhat monotonous. But if we're doing nothing that is important to us, the result will be that we will soon conclude—perhaps rightfully so—that we are unimportant people.

How often must it be done? Is it something we have to do daily? Weekly? Occasionally? Sometime? Perhaps not at all?

There are some things that we need to do regularly. They are the little molehills that will become mountains if they are not tended to on a timely basis. It may be a small thing—like eating—but if we don't do it regularly, the rest of life will go away.

Can someone else do it more effectively than I? Perhaps the answer is "No." Or again, it could be "Maybe." If the answer is "Yes," then perhaps this shouldn't be one of your goals at all. However, this introduces the whole area of delegation, a subject outside the scope of this book.[2]

Nevertheless, it is important to realize that too often we are doing things that we "like" to do only because we are accustomed to them. We know how to do them, like the Sunday School superintendent who, because he is also a musician, takes one-half hour each week to pick out the hymns for the following Sunday. If somebody else were doing the selecting, both parties would benefit.

Is it part of the larger task to which I am committed? This question relates our specific goals to our higher purpose. In his book, *The Systems Approach,* C. West Churchman[3] describes how necessary it is to ask the question, "Of what higher system is this system a part?"

In other words, what is the big picture? What is the meaning of it all? Only the Christian can give the ultimate answer to that question.

We should *expect* to find that our goals are related to a higher purpose. If we picture all of our goals as relationships to higher goals and purposes, we will discover that life becomes much more a whole. And at the same time we will be fitting into God's grand strategy for all of His church. If we cannot imagine how what we are doing fits into God's strategy, forget it!

Ask the question: *What will happen if it is not done at all?* Will there be a disaster? Trouble? Difficulty? Nothing? If the answer is nothing, maybe that's a clue to give it a low priority.

The American approach to problems is summed up in the proverb, "Never put off until tomorrow what you can do today." Europeans seem to take quite the opposite approach. Their view might be summed up, "Put off everything you can until tomorrow, for tomorrow you might not have to do it."

Both views, at various times, are undoubtedly correct! We need to decide which fits now.

Last, ask the question: *Is this the best way?* Is there a better goal that needs to be substituted for this one?

Suppose you have a goal to have everyone available four times to practice the Christmas pageant. But on reflection, you see that it could be broken down into three sub-group rehearsals of the choir, the actors and the reader. It's a much better way. And easier to manage, as well.

When we discuss personal planning we will have more to say about considering alternate solutions and thus finding optimum solutions.

Putting It Together—the ABC's

How does all this fit together? What might be a procedure that you could use to establish priorities for your different goals? Which goals come first? Which goals are more important?

Start by making a list of all the goals that you have considered. The list doesn't have to be in any particular order, but it is sometimes helpful to put them down in logical groups.

One way of dividing them up would be, say, by goals which had to do with relationships to others and goals which had to do with tasks. Some people like to make a list of all the things they would like to *be* and another of all the things they would like to *do.*

The result may be a very long list of goals. And there is nothing more frustrating or discouraging than to be presented with a long list of items and being asked to rank them in value, say, one through a hundred. The mind just can't hold all the information.

Besides, you are comparing each item with the other 99. And as soon as you have identified one goal as being number one, it automatically means that all the rest are less than one. And life doesn't work that way, does it?

69

There is no reason why we have to have *one* goal that is our top priority. We are much more likely to have a number of goals, all of which we consider "number one."

So, how do we handle such a long list?

There is a simple and effective way of sorting things out in terms of priorities. It has been around a long time and is surprisingly simple. It's called the *ABC technique*. Instead of trying to assign each goal a ranking number, assign it a value, an "A," "B" or "C."

A = "Must do" or very high value

B = "Should do" or medium value

C = "Can do" or low value

You can use the ABC technique in one of two ways. The first way is to go down your list and decide which of these goals you consider to be A goals. If it's a B or a C, go right past it. Just mark A's.

Now go back to the list and decide which ones are B goals. The rest are automatically C's.

A second way is to pause at each goal and decide whether you think it is an A, B or a C.

It does not matter which of these methods you use. Some people find one easier than the other.

Now go back and look at your list, regardless of which method you used. If you had a very long list, you may discover that you have too many A goals. We used to tell people to forget all those B's and C's because they would not have time for them. But then one of our friends put A next to all of his!

If you have too many A goals, then use the same ABC technique for all the A's. Ask the ABC question not in terms of all your goals, but just of these A goals. Subdivide the A goals into A-a, A-b and A-c.

You can see that what we are doing here is continually narrowing down the field. If you kept the process up, theoretically you would eventually arrive at just one A goal. It really works very nicely.

If you think about it, we are all doing our ABC's all the time. It is very much like Maslow's hierarchy of needs that we discussed earlier. As we sit on an airplane headed for home over Christmas holidays, our A priority may be to be with our family. If the aircraft crashes on the way, we may immediately shift to a new A, survival.

What we are doing here is recognizing this continuous process and consciously putting it to work. It's something we all do very well.

These, then, are techniques that you can use in sorting out your priorities. We recommend that you take a little time and test out this idea. You will find it useful in making all kinds of decisions. And we are going to discuss decisions in the next chapter.

Summing Up

Goals for which you have no priorities are useless. They will always be getting in the way of one another.

There are practical priority considerations that will help you work through the details of your value system. Choose the future instead of the past. Ask the questions: How important is it? How often must it be done? Can someone else do it more effectively than I? Is it part of a larger task to which I am committed? What will happen if it is not done at all? Is this the best way?

Instead of attempting to assign priorities to your goals on a one-by-one basis, first try dividing them up into major categories such as A—must do (high value), B—should do (medium value) and C—can do (low value).

Something for You to Do

In Figure A we have given you a list of 16 typical goals. Go through these, using the ABC technique and see how it works for you. Notice that we have given you two priority columns. If you end up with quite a few A's in your first try (Column 1),

71

PRIORITIZING WORKSHEET

Here are 16 personal goals for you to prioritize. For each one decide whether *for you* this is an A, B, or C. If you have more than three or four A's, try reprioritizing just the A's in column 2.

A—Very Important (high value)
B—Somewhat Important (medium value) ·
C—Not So Important (low value)

PERSONAL GOALS	Priority 1	Priority 2
1. Take the family out to dinner every ~~Wednesday~~ evening. *Friday*	B	
2. Read one book per week.	B	
3. Maintain membership on only three committees.	A	
4. Spend 15 minutes in prayer each day.	A	
5. Spend 15 minutes reading the Bible each day.	A	
6. Attend both Sunday school and church each Sunday.	A	
7. Take a class in counseling during the coming quarter.	B	
8. Learn to sail (or fly an airplane) by the end of this summer.	C	
9. Take 10 tennis lessons before November 30.	C	
10. Take a trip to the Holy Land (or Europe, Asia) next summer.	C	
11. Compliment at least one person each day.	B	
12. Make $_____ a year by the end of next year.	A	
13. Buy a sports car during the next 12 months.	C	
14. Tithe a minimum of 10% of my income.	A	
15. Build a house before next winter.	C	
16. Move to _Australia_ by the end of ~~next~~ *this* year.	A	

Figure A

perhaps you would like to take the second step and prioritize just your A's in Column 2.

Something for You to Do as a Family

Have each member of the family make a list of the purposes of your family life. Combine them all into one large list. Now have the family group go through the list using the ABC technique to establish areas of agreement or disagreement on what are the major purposes of your family.

You can do this in one of two ways. Have each member individually rank all of the goals in terms of ABC, and then compare lists and discuss them. Or, you can take an oral vote on each one as you go along, assigning an A only to those on which the entire family is agreed.

Footnotes

1. Ralph Neighbour summed up this matter very nicely by titling his book, *The Seven Last Words of the Church* (Grand Rapids: Zondervan, 1973).
2. For a discussion on delegation and other subjects relating to Christian leadership see Engstrom and Dayton, *The Art of Management for Christian Leaders* (Waco, TX: Word, 1976).
3. C. West Churchman, *The Systems Approach* (New York: Dell Books, 1969).

CHAPTER 8

YOU NEED TO MAKE DECISIONS

An important part of prioritizing is the process of making decisions. Deciding to do one thing often means that we are deciding not to do something else. We have to choose between alternatives.

One of the values of setting personal goals is that it forces us to make priority decisions. In fact, it forces us to the most important decisions we can make, decisions about our own lives.

You Can Decide

Many people go through life feeling that each major decision is traumatic. They picture themselves as procrastinators, people who just have difficulty making any decision. And yet most of them make many more decisions than they are aware of.

And probably, so do you. Which decisions did you make today? You decided what time to get up this morning. You decided what to wear. You decided what you would eat. You decided to read this book.

True, these may have been spur-of-the-moment decisions, but they were decisions, nevertheless. It is a fact that we *do* have control over most of our decisions even though, in one sense, it is impossible to make a decision about the future.

In fact, James implies that such thinking is completely presumptuous. "Come now, you who say, 'Today or tomorrow we will go into such and such a town and spend a year there and trade and get gain'; whereas you do not know about tomorrow. What is your life? For you are a mist that appears for a little time and then vanishes. Instead, you ought to say, 'If the Lord wills, we shall live and we shall do this or that' " (Jas. 4:13-15, *RSV*).

If the Lord wills. Our times *are* in His hands, but to recognize that fact and to act upon it is a decision in itself. And though we may not be able to control tomorrow, the decisions that we make today will have a tremendous effect upon us. James is not telling us to make no decisions, but to recognize that we need to make decisions in light of God's sovereignty. *Flexibility*

Be an Initiator

We need to strive to be *pro-active,* to be initiators, rather than to continually be reacting as responders to the situation around us. If we wait until we are forced to a decision, too often the decision can only be yes or no, go or don't go. That is why we need to set a goal for the future, so we will open to ourselves the possibility of alternatives.

We need to look ahead to future goals. The more time we have, the more alternatives there are. It is surprising how often we fail to see this.

We are faced with a decision, perhaps an opportunity for a new job in another city. The apparent question is, "Will we take the job?" This is based on some other questions: "Are we willing to leave our present job and our present home?"

76

"Would we rather work for the new company than work for our present company?"

But as soon as we have made a decision that we would be willing to leave our present location, we open ourselves up to a whole range of other alternatives. Once we realize that there is perhaps a better situation for us in another locality, then we should consider not only the opportunity offered to us, but all the other opportunities that may lie alongside it.

The next time you are faced with a decision to substitute one goal for another (move or stay), ask yourself what other goals you might have if you are willing to give up the first one.

The decisions we make reflect on our goals. When we recognize that there is more than one possible outcome, we are in effect recognizing that we might have more than one desirable goal.

Decisions Can Be Changed

Recognize that very few decisions are irrevocable. Most of them can be changed. Perhaps the decision we make to accept Christ is the only permanent decision of our life.

Have you made a decision to go somewhere? Can you not just as easily make another decision not to go?

Perhaps a year ago you made a decision to set out on a certain course of action. When people questioned you about it, perhaps you responded, "But I made a *decision!*" Very good. Now make another decision to change that course!

It All Adds Up to Experience

One of the marks of a good decision-maker is that he or she has the ability to put past "mistakes" to work. He or she recognizes that life is full of bad decisions.

"The story is told of a crusty old bank president who was about to retire. The board of directors had passed over a number of older men and had chosen a fast-rising young executive as his replacement.

77

"One morning the young president-to-be made an appointment with his predecessor to seek some advice. 'Mr. Adams,' he said, 'as you know, I lack a great deal of the qualifications you already have for this job. You have been very successful as president of this bank. I wondered if you would care to share with me some of the insights you have gained, those things which you believe have been the key to your success?'

"Adams fixed him with his bushy-browed stare and replied, 'Young man, two words: good decisions!'

" 'Thank you very much, sir. But how does one make good decisions?' replied the younger man.

" 'One word, young man: experience!'

" 'But how does one get experience?'

" 'Two words, young man: bad decisions!' "[1]

If you are lost in the woods with no idea of where you are, and you see a fire lookout tower up on a hill, as a sensible person you will make a decision to start moving toward that tower. Now, it may well be that as you head for the tower, you may encounter a stream which you cannot cross. You will have to change your plans, make a new decision to move down the stream to find another place where you can cross. As you keep moving toward the tower, you may suddenly come across a well-known path leading home which will completely change your initial decision to move toward the tower.

Small decisions to move in a new direction, toward a new goal, are much easier to make when we see that they are changeable.

Decide! Make a decision! And when you have made a decision, be proud of it. "Hey, look! I just made a decision!" And when the time comes to change that decision, be proud of that too.[2] Making decisions about your life is the stuff that life is made of.

Summing Up

In order to prioritize, in order to begin to manage our life, we have to decide to do it. We have much more control over decisions of life than most of us are aware. We can decide. Most decisions are not irrevocable. They can be changed. All of life is made up of "good decisions" and "bad decisions," the sum total of which is *experience!*

Something for You to Do

Make a list of all of the decisions you made today. Which ones gave you difficulty? Why?

Make a list of decisions you wish you had not made. As you look them over, are they revocable?

As you look at the decisions that face you in the immediate future, which of these would have been easier to make a month ago, or a year ago?

Footnotes

1. Edward R. Dayton, *Tools for Time Management* (Grand Rapids: Zondervan, 1974).
2. For a detailed treatment of the decision-making process, particularly as it is related to problem-solving, see Kepner and Tregoe, *The Rational Manager* (New York: McGraw-Hill, 1965), p. 64f.

CHAPTER 9

PRIORITIES AND CHRISTIAN COMMITMENT

"I'd like to help, Pastor, but that's not one of my priorities."

The pastor didn't really want to hear that answer from Jim, but there wasn't any way he could have responded, he thought, as he hung up the telephone. "Not one of my priorities." What was Jim really saying? What *are* priorities?

We noted earlier that all priority questions are essentially *when* questions. For example, if we have 10 very important things we want to do, the priority question is, "Which one of these will we do first?" But given a list of 100 things to do, we all recognize that there are *some* things which we will never do. Priorities, then, have to do with what we *want* to do—our goals. What our pastor never found out from Jim was what things took a *higher* priority than what he had asked Jim to do, for he never asked what goals Jim had that were more important.

Like goals without plans, "priorities" without goals to prioritize are just so much language, more verbal fog.

Priorities Have to Do with Values

What goals we choose, and what priorities we give to them, are a reflection of our values or what we call a value system. But what *is* a value system? When asked to describe our value system, most of us feel somewhat embarrassed. We recognize that we should have such a system, but we have probably never been asked to describe it.

Your real value system is reflected by what you do. In spite of the fact that most Christians are very belief-oriented, we are what we *do*, not what we believe. What we believe may eventually change what we *do*, but for the moment our actions reflect our value system.

How can you discover your own value system? In their excellent book, *Values Clarification*,[1] the authors point out that the best way to discover your values is to give yourself a number of choices and see which ones you would prefer. You might write down all of your purposes in life and then use the ABC technique (Chapter 7) to decide which of these you would place at the top of the list. By then asking yourself *why* you have given high priority to some items and low priority to others, you can get in touch with your real motivators, your real values.

Most Christians would say that their value system must certainly have its roots in the authority of God's Word. If nothing else then, we should look to the Bible to discover our basis for deciding which things should come first. The difficulty is that the Bible is always viewed through the lens of our own culture.

Whether we acknowledge it or not, we have a way of deciding what is right and what is wrong in terms of what our own culture is telling us. For example, 25 years ago very few women would be seen in a church without wearing a hat. They would be following the biblical injunction that women's heads

82

should be covered in a house of worship (see 1 Cor. 11:10).

Why is it that 25 years later in most Protestant churches very few women wear hats? Why, there hasn't even been an article written on the subject that we know of! And yet somehow we have agreed with our culture that ladies don't have to wear hats in church. This small example demonstrates the continual need to search back to basic primary considerations, the value system of the Bible.

Our situation will always be changing. The *meaning* of an action today may be quite different from the meaning of an action 10 years from now. Without seeming to pick on women, but to use another illustration, if a woman came to church in a miniskirt in 1947, it would have meant something entirely different than when a woman came to church in a miniskirt in 1967.[2]

The Three Levels of Christian Commitment

Where do we begin? How can we work our way out of a mass of detail and attempt to find a *Christian* priority system? If we are going to attempt this business of setting goals for our lives, goals against which we can try to express our faith as to what God wants us to do and to be, then those goals should be able to stand up against the test of God's Word.

In trying to understand any problem or question, a good way to begin is to divide it up into smaller parts. Let us take this approach as we attempt to establish a Christian priority system. We believe the Bible gives us three broad levels of priority:

First, our commitment to God and Christ;

Second, our commitment to the Body of Christ, His Church;

Third, commitment to the work of Christ, the task God gives us to do.   Family ?

As Christians, we agree that the Bible teaches us to establish God in Christ as our first or highest priority. For commitment to Christ is more important than our commitment to men and women, even our brothers and sisters in Christ. And our commitment to those same brothers and sisters is more important than our commitment to the work of Christ.

Yet time and time again, we have seen both Christian "professionals" and Christian laymen exchange the second and third priorities. They have become so involved with the *work* of Christ that they have gone right past the second biblical priority of commitment to the Body.

Another way of expressing these biblical priorities is to recognize that we need time *alone* with God, time with God *through His Body* and, thirdly, time with God *in the work*.

But are these really the priorities of commitment that the Bible gives? Let's see.

Level One. Jesus said that there was no way to God except through Him (see John 14:6). He said that as many as believed that He was the Christ were given the power to become God's sons and daughters (see John 1:12). He put commitment to Himself higher than any other possible relationship. If a man was not willing to leave father and mother, sister and brother for Him, then his commitment was less than whole (see Matt. 10:37-39). "He that is not with me is against me" (Matt. 12:30). "You cannot serve two masters" (Matt. 6:24, *TLB*).

Level Two. But what about this second level of commitment, commitment to the Body of Christ? Does it really come before the work of Christ?

It is interesting that the Bible gives us few direct *measurements* of our commitment. But one that we hear over and over is this: the real measure of our Christianity is our love for each other. Jesus thought this was important enough to call it a new commandment. "A new commandment I give unto you, that ye love one another" (John 13:34). "This is how all men will know that you are my disciples, because you have such love for one another" (John 13:35, *Phillips*).

In His high priestly prayer of John 17, Jesus exclaimed to the Father that men would know that these were His disciples, if they exhibited the same love for one another that existed between Him and His Father (see John 17:21-23). This relationship is not a choice, but a *given*.

The eye cannot say to the hand, "I have no need of you" (1 Cor. 12:21 *RSV*). The day you became a Christian you became part of an indissoluble Body. You are stuck with us, and we are stuck with you!

Paul in his letters has very little to say about evangelism. He only uses the word "evangelism" or "evangelistic" three times. The major thrust of Paul's letters is relationships between Christians.

— Wife + children come before "brothers" + "sisters"

Jesus came to change *relationships.* He came first to change the relationship between the individual and the Father. But He always assumes that the outworking of this renewed fellowship is also going to result in a new kind of relationship between all those who name His Father as their Father.

Righteousness has to do with relationships. If you were the only person in the world, it would be very difficult to commit an unrighteous act. Most of the loving of God that we do, we do by loving men and women. Most of the sinning we do against God, we do by sinning against our fellow men and women.

The first eleven chapters of Romans build a foundation on which our relationships to each other, ethics, can operate. The Bible has much more to say about *what I should be* (relationships) than *what I should do* (work).

Only when this second relationship is well understood, and our commitment to it is well made, can we really move on to the work of Christ.

Level Three. What is the "work of Christ"? When we speak of this as being the third priority after our commitment to Christ and our commitment to the Church, what do we mean?

One way of thinking about this third priority is to compare the two major tasks of the Church. The first of these is what we have come to call "nurture," building up the Body for the ministry (see Eph. 4:11,12). The other part of the work of the Church is to "go forth," to evangelize, to visit those in prison, to care for widows, to give a cup of cold water in Jesus' name, to have compassion upon the hungry and the poor. These are all part of the "going forth."

How will the work get done? As we build our relationships within the Body, on the strong foundation of our relationship to God in Christ, we will discover that there is a natural base on which we can do the work of Christ (see Fig. A).

3. WORK OF CHRIST
2. BODY OF CHRIST
1. COMMITMENT TO CHRIST

Figure A

There will be some who will immediately object that if we spend all of our time in relating to one another, we may never get around to doing the work of Christ. They are right. A struggle must always go on.[3]

Perhaps St. Augustine summed the matter up best when he said, "Love God and do as you please." If we love the Lord with all our mind and all our body and all our strength, and our neighbor as ourselves, there is little doubt that what we want to do will be what Christ wants us to do.

Two more observations are needed: First, no Christian can assume that because he has worked on the first two priorities he may be excused from the third. To be a Christian is to be involved in all three. Second, the second two priorities (and all the rest of the Christian life) are based on the power given through the primary relationship to God in Christ.

What About the Rest of My Life?

"Well, that's fine," you may say. "But what about all the rest of my life? Do these three priorities cover *everything?*"

No, they don't. There is a great deal of living to do that may be very difficult to fit into these three priorities. The grass needs to be mowed, the dishes need to be washed, we need to earn a living. But as we try to align our total life purpose and the goals which issue forth from that purpose in a God-ward direction, we need some way to sort all this out. We will discuss the practical working out of this kind of priority system in Part IV, which covers planning.[4]

If you haven't made a commitment to God and Christ, make it now! If you have, recognize that this commitment has brought you into a new relationship, not only with the Father, but with those who call themselves Christians. Center your purpose and goals in these two relationships and with these as a foundation, move on to doing His work. Making your commitment to God your key motivation can revolutionize your life. It can take the emphasis off doing, and place it on being. It can bring you into a new fellowship with your Lord, with your family, with others.

God *will* get *His* work done. Part of His grand design is that His love should be demonstrated among men and the power of that love, in turn, would change the world. When the "work" becomes more important than people, we are denying both God's power and His sovereignty. We then fall back into doing that work in the strength of ourselves rather than the strength of His Spirit.

Summing Up

The Christian should set his goals in light of three levels or expressions of commitment: First, commitment to the Christ; second, commitment to the Body of Christ; and third, commitment to the work of Christ. Each of these naturally flows out of the one that comes before it.

These three aspects of our commitment do not cover everything we do in life, but they form the basis of a Christian value system.

Something for You to Do

Take a look at your datebook for the last week or mentally review what you did during the week. Try to sort out these events under the three levels of commitment: (1) to the Christ; (2) to the Body of Christ; (3) to the work of Christ.

In light of what you have noted, did you live a balanced Christian life last week? Where does it appear that your top priorities really lie?

Footnotes

1. Simon, Howe and Kirschenbaum, *Values Clarification* (New York: Hart Publishing Co., 1972).
2. For a good discussion on the need to continually review our actions in light of the Bible *and* our culture, see Gene Getz's *Sharpening the Focus of the Church* (Chicago: Moody Press, 1974).
3. For a good discussion on the working out of this tension, read Elizabeth O'Connor's *Journey Inward, Journey Outward* (New York: Harper and Row, 1968), the story of the Church of the Saviour, Washington, D.C.
4. For an illustration of the outworking of these three levels of commitment in the life of a local church, read Raymond C. Ortlund's *Lord, Make My Life a Miracle* (Ventura, CA: Regal Books, 1974).

PART IV PLANNING

GOALS

STRATEGY
FOR
LIVING

LIVING

PRIORITIES

PLANNING

10   You Need to Plan
11   How to Do Personal Planning

CHAPTER 10

YOU NEED TO PLAN

Goals, priorities and planning. It's very easy for goals just to be daydreams. "Someday I will . . ." can be a fantasy that never becomes a reality. In order to make your goal operational, you need a way to accomplish it. You need a plan.

It is not a question of whether we will or will not plan. To make no plans is a plan in itself. Rather, it is a question of whether we will affect the future with purpose or at random. "The new man . . . is out to learn what he ought to be, according to the plan of God" (Col. 3:10, *Phillips*). We have a responsibility to decide what God wants us to be and what He wants us to do, and therefore we have a responsibility to plan.

Planning Saves Time

How strange it is that many of us who recognize the crucial need for planning in our church, business or profession, never apply planning concepts to our personal life. For in the same way that planning saves time (and a great deal of money and energy) in an organization, so it will save time for ourselves. Within obvious limits, there is a direct relationship between the amount of time we spend planning and the effectiveness in reaching our goal.

As the diagram in Figure A shows, the more time we spend planning, the more effective we will be in carrying out our plans.

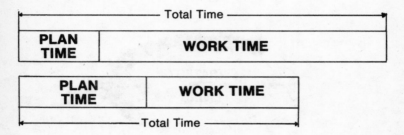

Figure A

We experience this every day: "If I had only thought to bring that tool, this job would be a cinch." "Why didn't I remember I had to take Jimmy for a haircut? Now I will have to make two trips." "Why Mabel, I thought *you* were bringing the lunch!"

Many people think they just don't have time for planning. They tend to be activists, people who want to get on with it. But if there is no planning, then we will probably do the first thing that comes to our mind whether it is effective or not. The most effective people are those who have trained themselves to think (plan) before they act. If someone rushes in with a "We've only got ten minutes to . . ." your best response is, "Okay, let's take three minutes to plan."

What Is Planning?

Planning is trying to discover how to accomplish our goals.

92

There may be many ways to reach the goal. The question before us is what is the best way.

Planning is moving from the "now" to the "then," from the way things are to the way we want them to be. Like goals, plans are statements of faith, for they have to do with the future.

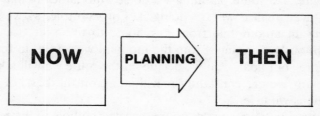

Figure B

In Figure B we have shown planning as an arrow. It points a direction. It is a road map toward the future, one upon which we can constantly improve as we move toward that future.

It's a way of thinking about the future before the future happens. Notice we said that it is a way of *thinking* about the future. That's the nice thing about planning; we can imagine what the future is going to be like and take those steps which will be more likely to give us satisfaction and less likely to give us dissatisfaction.

Plans Are Changeable

But let's face it, some people do not like to plan. One of the reasons some people dislike "planning" is they conceive it as making a rigid and predetermined set of decisions as to what they are going to do in the future. They believe a plan is something that *must* be carried out. Or they become so enamored with their plans they can't give them up. As the writer of Proverbs said, "It is pleasant to see plans develop. That is why fools refuse to give them up even when they are wrong" (Prov. 13:19, *TLB*).

Plans, whether they are personal plans or organizational

93

plans, should always make provision for continuous evaluation. We should plan, take the first step, look back (get feedback) and look forward, and reevaluate what is going on. If the plan is still good, fine. If it is not, let's change it.

We find this kind of feedback in almost everything we do in daily life. Yet some planning we do so automatically that we don't even realize we are doing it. For example, as we are driving an automobile from our home to the store, we are continuously planning. From the moment we set out to reach the store—our goal—and we decide on the route we will take—our plan—we are constantly reevaluating on the basis of the situations we face.

Some situations, such as an unexpected pothole in the road, require an instant change of plan—a quick jerk of the steering wheel. Others, such as an accident at an intersection that is backing up traffic, cause us to make a more calculated change of plan and take a different route to the store. Of course, we don't expect to change our big plans from moment to moment, but we should expect that they will change, for the future is seldom like we expect it to be.

Plans Help Communicate

Planning helps us move toward goals, but planning helps in many other ways as well. Planning is a way of communicating our intentions to ourselves and to others. "Can two walk together, except they be agreed?" (Amos 3:3). Unless you have decided where you are going, how can I decide to accompany you?

Understanding God's Strategy

For the Christian, planning is trying to understand God's will and responding to that understanding by our actions.

We need to keep reminding ourselves that plans, like goals, are statements about the future, and for the Christian any statement about the future is a statement of faith.

Planning Is Like Problem Solving

Planning is a way of seeking alternate and thus optimum solutions to reaching our goal or solving a problem. In this sense, planning is very much like problem solving. We assume that we can reach the goal; we also assume that just as there are many roads that may lead to our destination, so there might be many ways in which we could reach our goal. Knowing that something will not work is just as valuable as knowing what will work. Better to "fail" on paper than in practice.[1]

We need to plan, but we need to see planning as a tool, not as an end in itself. There is a tension about plans. Some people love to plan. We can get so wrapped up in planning (which is basically thinking about tomorrow) that we do not live today. Somehow the tension between being a "today person" and a "tomorrow person" needs to be continually worked on. It's never resolved.

Summing Up

If we are going to reach our goals, then we need to decide *how* we are going to reach them. We need a plan. Planning saves time. Planning is selecting from a number of alternates to try to find the best way. Planning is trying to understand God's will and to respond to that understanding by our actions.

Something for You to Do

List five goals that you have for which you have no plans. These might include everything from having dinner ready at six o'clock to making a big business decision. Note which of these might be more likely to happen if you had a plan.

Footnotes

1. For a more detailed analysis of problem-solving and its relationship to planning, see Edward R. Dayton's *God's Purpose/Man's Plans* (Monrovia, CA: MARC, 1972). See also Charles H. Kepner and B. B. Tregoe, *The Rational Manager* (New York: McGraw-Hill, 1965).

CHAPTER 11

HOW TO DO PERSONAL PLANNING

When making plans, you have to start with a goal. If you don't know where you're going, any road will take you there. What is it that you want to do or to be? Picture the situation as you want it to be.

It may be that you will have to start with a purpose and then break this down into goals, all of which may contribute toward that one purpose. It may even be—as we will see later—that you have to make a plan to plan.

Describe Your Situation

Describe as best you can the situation as you understand it. There are two specific factors in your present situation you might want to consider: the forces *helping* and the forces *hindering* the situation.

PLANNING WORKSHEET

STEP 2 PRESENT SITUATION	STEP 3 FORCES HELPING	STEP 3 FORCES HINDERING	STEP 4 STEPS TO GOAL	STEP 1 MY GOAL
We don't seem to have enough uninterrupted time to share where we're at.	Desire to be with her.	Kids interrupt us. Conflicting schedules. Not enough time.	1. Discover what she would like. 2. Put date on calendar. 3. Ask secretary for help.	To spend two hours a week alone with my wife.
Reading 4 or 5 books.	Desire to do a better job.	No regular program. No specific reading goals. T.V. News—papers. Not enough time. Read too slow.	1. Decide on types of books I want to read. 2. Estimate number of pages in twenty books. 3. Estimate my reading speed. 4. Figure outline needed. 5. Decide on most optimum block of time. 6. Set it aside. Protect it. _or_ Think of time to use that are now wasted.	To read twenty books this year.

Figure A

In his "force field analysis," Kurt Lewin[1] suggests that seeing a situation in the light of helping and hindering forces is an excellent way to analyze a problem. We agree.

To see how all this works, let's look at the two examples in the planning form in Figure A.

The Case of the Lonely Husband

Roger Jensen had a new goal: he wanted to spend two hours a week alone with his wife. It was part of his larger purpose to be a more effective husband. He decided that as part of this purpose he wanted to have more quality time with her. So he wrote down in the right-hand column: "To spend two hours a week alone with my wife, beginning next week."

He then set about analyzing his present situation in the left-hand column: "We don't seem to have enough uninterrupted time to share where we're at." He noted under "Forces Helping" that he had a desire to be with her. Then under "Forces Hindering" he noted that the kids kept interrupting them; they had conflicting schedules and there just didn't seem to be enough time.

With this information in hand, Roger started working through steps toward his goal. His first step was to "discover what she would like." That's a pretty good idea. Certainly if they were going to have some quality time together, they ought to know what kind of time it should be. Next, he decided to make some specific dates on the calendar and protect them in advance.

But Roger knew very well that his past history indicated he often didn't keep all the appointments he made, so he wrote down, "3: Ask secretary for help." This was a wise move. We all need to hold ourselves accountable for the things we want to do, and by asking his secretary to remind him of his weekly date with his wife—which for Roger and his wife, Mary, was a weekly luncheon together—he took a final step toward making his goal a habit.

The Case of the "Crash Course" Manager

Bud Barnes was a manager in a middle-sized engineering firm. He had been promoted because of technical ability, but he discovered that there was a great deal to be learned about this business of management that he had not been taught in college.

As he thought through his long-range goals, one of his shorter-range supporting goals turned out to be that he decided he should read 20 management books during the coming year. He pulled out his sheet of paper and wrote in the right-hand side "To read 20 management books this year." (See worksheet example, Fig. A.)

Then he began to take a look at his present situation. As best he could tell he was reading no more than four or five books of all kinds in one year.

When he looked for "Forces Helping" him to move toward his goal, he knew that he had a desire to do a better job. The "Forces Hindering" seemed to be that he had no regular reading program, no specific reading goals. TV and newspapers kept taking up his time. He also concluded that he was a slow reader. What could he do?

Bud started working on some steps toward the goal. Like Roger Jensen, he recognized that the first step he had to take was to analyze exactly what it was he wanted to do, what type of books he wanted to read. He decided that after he had compiled such a list, a second step would be to estimate the number of pages in those 20 books. A third step for Bud was to estimate his reading speed. This in turn led him to step four, which was to find out how much time he was going to need to read all of those pages.

For the moment he put aside the idea of trying to learn to read faster.[2] Instead he planned to take step five of blocking out some optimum reading time. The final step of his plan was to put this time down on his calendar and to protect it and to think of other ways he might fit in reading time during the week.

Planning *Is* Like Problem Solving

As you may have already detected in the two examples just given, the planning worksheet actually gives you a practical approach to problem solving. There is usually a close relationship between planning and problem solving. Planning can help you reach a goal or solve a problem.

In fact, a good way to look at a problem is to see it as a deviation or detour from reaching a goal. To see how this works, let's look at what might happen when someone uses the planning worksheet to solve a personal problem.

The Case of the Concerned Mother

Clare Johnson had a personal problem. Her fifteen-year-old daughter, Christy, was going through that counter-dependent stage of life. What had, up until a few months ago, been a close relationship between mother and daughter was now becoming more and more strained.

Clare's immediate problem was that she was concerned with Christy's dating habits. Christy had announced that she had a big date with a friend by the name of Alan next Saturday night and she wanted permission to stay out until two in the morning.

As Clare thought about her problem, she asked herself, "What goals are involved here? What is it I really want for Christy?"

She knew that her *purpose* in her relationship with Christy was to help her make her own decisions and become a mature person. Clare also recognized that she had another purpose: As a mother she wanted to maintain communication with her daughter, to be a restraining influence as well as an encouraging influence where it was needed. As she thought about these two purposes, she concluded that her goal was to make sure Christy would understand her concern. If at all possible she wanted to let Christy make her own decisions.

What were some of the alternatives? Clare could forbid Christy to go, but that would really only solve the immediate

101

problem. She could insist that she talk to Alan's mother first, but that would make Christy feel more like a child than an adult. She could plan conflicting family programs for the same date. But that would be both dishonest to herself and to Christy.

Finally, Clare took out a sheet of paper and worked out the plan shown in Figure B. The means she used to communicate with Christy was an "I-message." "Christy, if you did not come home until two o'clock on Sunday morning, I know that I would feel very upset. I really don't know Alan, and you've never stayed out past twelve before. What can you do to help me?"[3]

Clare hoped that her daughter would offer an alternative solution and from this they might work out an arrangement with which they were both happy. If the alternative solution was not acceptable, Clare would have to rest in the hope that Christy would feel more loved because her mother was exercising her judgment and authority.

Roger, Bud and Clare—we've shown you three examples of working out a planning sheet. But that's still not the whole process. After you do a planning sheet, you still need to ask two very important questions.

Is It Practical?

Once you have arrived at what appears to be a good plan in terms of steps to be taken, the final question is, "Is it practical?" You need to calculate the amount of time, money and effort that will be needed for each step.

Only after you have added up the total resources needed, and have ascertained that they are indeed available, do you have a *workable* plan.

Do I Have to Replan?

Suppose your ideas don't add up? Perhaps they cost too much or are just impractical, and you discover you have a plan

PLANNING WORKSHEET

STEP 2 PRESENT SITUATION	STEP 3 FORCES HELPING	STEP 3 FORCES HINDERING	STEP 4 STEPS TO GOAL	STEP 1 MY GOAL
1. Christy wants to go out with Alan, stay out until 12 o'clock. 2. Don't know Al.	Christy's growing need for independence.	Christy never stayed out after 12 o'clock before.	1. Under what circumstance would I be willing to have Christy stay out until 2 o'clock. 2. Sort out my own feelings so that I can express my problem and and an "I message." 3. Share my concern with Christy and my need to be reassured of her well-being. 4. Make a decision.	Purpose 1. Maintain communication with Christy. 2. Be a restraining influence as well as encouraging influence. Goal Help Christy to make a decision acceptable to both Alan and Christy.

Figure B

that won't work? Don't be discouraged. Even with failures you can make valuable progress.

Thomas Edison worked long and hard in his laboratory doing experiment after experiment in an attempt to find the right filament for the incandescent electric light. On a particular day he had just completed his ten thousandth experiment only to discover another way that wouldn't work. When he arrived home from his laboratory that night, he shared this bit of news with his wife.

"Aren't you pretty discouraged, Tom?" she asked.

"Discouraged?" responded Edison. "Certainly not! I now know 10,000 ways that won't work!"

Experimenting on paper can sometimes save an awful lot of work in the laboratory of life. Better to fail in the planning than in the execution. Your first plan (or plans) can lead you to alternative plans that will succeed. As you find alternatives, you will reach your goal or solve your problem.

Where Do You Get "Alternative Plans"?

Someone has aptly noted that the cleanliness of theory is no match for the mess of reality. If we start doing our planning within the context of where we are right now, we may soon give up.

Somehow we have to take our mind away from the negative situation at hand and draw from both our experience and the experience of others all of the different ideas that may be there. If you're stuck in some quicksand, there is little use in analyzing its consistency. Better to look for a nearby branch!

For the moment, we need to ignore the problem of the present and consider the possibilities of the future. There are a number of ways of doing this:

The Random List. Some people prefer to sit down with a blank sheet and just list out all the ideas that come to them in any random fashion. Then they go back and try to order these in some logical way, eliminating the ones that won't work.

104 *Brainstorming*

Brainstorming

The Slip Technique. Others find that the *slip technique* works well. On a batch of 3x5 cards or—less expensive!—slips of paper, write down every idea you have. Pay no attention to logic or what has gone before. Later on, spread these written ideas out on a table and arrange them in ways which will work into a usable plan.

This process has the double benefit of showing gaps in thinking, gaps which can prompt us to identify new ways of filling in missing steps. This approach also works very well as a brainstorming technique with other people, say, the members of your own family.

Here's an example:

Remember the family that was disappointed in their vacation? Their disappointment was the result of not having communicated their personal goals for the vacation. Suppose they had taken another tack? Suppose they had sat down around the dining room table, each one with a small pile of slips in front of him.

Dad might have said, "All right, what is it we want to get out of this vacation?"

Junior might have replied, "Learn to water ski!"

To which Dad might have responded, "Fine, write that down!" And with this Junior could have written down his own idea on his own slip of paper.

"What else do we want to get out of this vacation?"

"Well, I'm hoping for a good rest from cooking," Mother might have replied.

"Fine, write that down!" should be Dad's response. "As each person goes through thinking of all the things he/she might want on the vacation and writes down his/her ideas, the family will probably discover that they are building on each other's ideas and can eventually plan a vacation which is acceptable to them all. Or, as an alternative, do it one way this year with the promise of doing it another way next year.

This slip technique will work for idea gathering whether

you're planning a vacation, thinking about your honeymoon, listing characteristics of the kind of person you would like to become. The secret is to take every idea as it comes, without judgment and—hopefully—without comment, then do your evaluating later.

Plan Time for Planning

Planning *does* take time, but it's worth it. We need to set aside time to plan on our calendar, or we may never get into the habit of doing it.

How often should you plan? In terms of reviewing your Life Goals Statement (which we'll discuss in Chapter 14), you should replan at least once a year. Goals and plans that lie a year ahead should probably be reviewed every three months. Monthly plans should be reviewed each week.

Use a "Things-to-Do" List

No one seems to have come up with a better way of managing the minutia of life than making a daily "Things-to-Do" list—which is nothing more than a random list of all the things you plan to do this day. By noting in one place everything you have to do, you get a picture of your whole day.

A "Things-to-Do" list helps integrate your different daily needs. You can group some things such as telephone calls or note that you can combine a trip to the market with a trip to pick up the kids at school. You can remember birthdays that need a friendly greeting and, generally, lay out the progress of life.

But if making a list is going to become a habit, it must first get down on your calendar. So plan 10 minutes for it at the beginning or end of each day, a half hour at the end of each week, perhaps two hours each month. (See page 170 for another example.)

Big Plans, Little Plans

This approach to planning—the making of lists—is useful in

planning for both big goals and smaller ones. You will soon discover that big plans lead to the need for smaller plans. For example, when working on a big plan for a new career you should first list all of the major steps. These major steps can then in themselves become goals for which you can make more detailed, smaller plans.

Pray over your plans. Expect that the Holy Spirit is going to put into your mind alternatives for better goals. For the Christian, thoughtful, personal planning and devotional time are linked very closely. Don't be surprised if in the midst of your praying you are suddenly struck with a new solution to a nagging problem or another alternative for the future. How else can God communicate with you in prayer? "A man's mind plans his way, but the Lord directs his steps" (Prov. 16:9, RSV).

Summing Up

To make a plan take these steps (review worksheet example, Fig. A):

1. Identify—write out—your goal.
2. Describe your situation (or the problem).
3. List "Forces Helping" and "Forces Hindering" you.
4. List specific steps you plan to take toward your goal.

After working out your plan, ask two more important questions:

Is it practical?

Do I have to replan?

Failure is a way to success, as you find alternatives. You can get alternative plans by using the random list or the slip technique.

Planning takes time but it's worth it. One of the best tools for making daily plans is the "Things-to-Do" list. When making any plans—big or little—take time to pray.

Something for You to Do

From the planning worksheet examples in this chapter,

make your own copy of the form and try filling it in with your own plan. Choose some goal with which you are very familiar. It may even be one you have already achieved. In the "goal" column write down a clear goal statement, one that is accomplishable and measurable. In the proper columns, state the "Present Situation," the "Forces Helping" and "Forces Hindering." Now attempt to write down the steps needed to reach the goal. Do this for a number of different areas for your life.

Something for the Family to Do

As a family or as husband and wife, choose a goal for which you would like to plan. Write it in the "goal" column. In the left-hand column write down what you believe the situation to be and next gather the information—perhaps using the slip technique—to write down the "Forces Helping" or "Forces Hindering." Use the slip technique to gather ideas on all of the steps that might take you toward the plan.

Now sort out the most useful ideas and write a plan. For each step of the plan estimate the date when it can be accomplished. Estimate the cost and time for taking each step.

Calculate whether this is a practical plan. If it doesn't seem practical or costs too much, rejoice! You now know one way that won't work. Go back and try another alternative.

Footnotes

1. Kurt Lewin, *Field Theory in Social Science.* Cartwright Dorwin, ed. (Westport, CT: Greenwood Press, 1975).
2. If Bud had wanted to read faster, we would have recommended Ben E. Johnson's *Rapid Reading with a Purpose* (Glendale, CA: Regal Books, 1973).
3. If *you* are having trouble in this area, Haim Ginott's *Between Parent and Child* (New York: Avon, 1969) has helped many parents.

PART V LIVING

12   Living All of Life
13   Living a Strategic Life

CHAPTER 12

LIVING ALL OF LIFE

Any discussion about goal setting and establishing priorities that deals with only one portion of our life is bound to fail. We cannot separate that which we do at the office from that which we do at home, or that which we do with our children from that which we do at church. Life is a whole. Activity in each area will impact on every other. Those who attempt to live a compartmentalized life are continually forced to juggle their priorities. They end up being one person in one situation and another person in another situation.

A person who pictures his business or work, even his work with a Christian organization, as having an entirely different set of priorities from his home life, will be in constant conflict. If for the third evening in a row he has to call home and tell his wife that he is going to be late again, there is probably something wrong with his priorities.

We know many Christian leaders who can give personal

testimony to the damaged lives that have resulted from a father whose "work for the Lord" was so important that his children, his family, had to take second place. The same thing can happen to a professional woman and even to the woman whose ministry centers around her home. Her house and her children can so compete for her attention that her husband is relegated to someone who happens to live there.

We need to deal with the *whole person*.

In the same way that body and spirit are integrally one, so are all the different roles of our life. We need to see each area in respect to every other area. We need to see each relationship in respect to every other relationship. How we relate to our children, how we relate to our spouse, how we relate to our work, how we relate to our church are all part of the whole.

Living life apart from this concept of the whole person is hopeless.

Picture the Whole Person

But how different we all are! Of the some eight billion people who have ever lived, no two have ever been completely alike, not even "identical" twins. What a fantastic concept!

Each of us is made up of a number of different "beings." Each one of us is a spiritual being, an intellectual being, a physical being, an emotional being.

Some of us are thinkers. Others are doers. Some of us are teachers. Others are learners. One may be a follower. Another is more comfortable in leading. And that is all right. God created us that way.

The amazing thing is that God not only loves you, He *likes* you just as you are right now! Oh, He may not like everything you do or everything you think, but His love looks past all of those things and sees the redeemed person. That is why Paul could so confidently affirm, "If a man is in Christ he becomes a new person altogether—the past is finished and gone, everything has become fresh and new" (2 Cor. 5:17, *Phillips*).

112

Yet even in Christ, each one of us lives a different life. Each one of us is made up of a different *history*, lives in a different *situation*, has different *commitments* and obligations and has different needs and *goals*. We might picture ourselves as being in the center of our history, our present situation, our present commitments and our future goals (Fig. A).

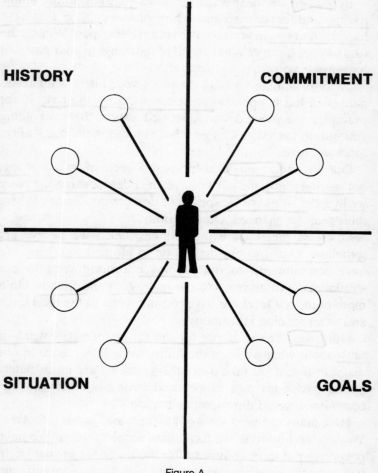

HISTORY

COMMITMENT

SITUATION

GOALS

Figure A

4 Dimensions of Life

In this diagram we have tried to picture these four dimensions that affect us all. These are the dimensions that make each of our lives so different. We have purposely drawn our diagram so that the person in the center can be seen as suspended between all the dimensions of his or her personal history, commitment, situation and future goals.

By *history* we mean such things as past education, ethnic background, experience and a host of other things that have happened to you in your own or your parents' past. What is the sum of your history? What are all of the things in your past that have made you what you are today?

There is nothing you can do about your history. What has happened has happened—you cannot change the past. If, for example, you grew up with a poor education, there is nothing you can do to change that fact. But you can make plans to get more and better training.[1]

Our present *situation* is comprised of such things as our age, our marital status, the job we have, the titles we carry, the place we live, the language we speak—or don't speak. Some of these things can be changed. Others cannot.

Our *commitments* are those things which we believe are somehow related to our dedication to life and to others. We have commitments to our employer, commitments to our employees, commitments to our colleagues and friends. On a more mundane level, we have commitments to the local bank and other lending institutions!

Our *goals* are our hopes for the future, our statements of faith about what we want the future to be like. Notice in our diagram that if we take away the goals, we are immediately pulled back into past history and strung out between our commitments and our present situation.

How many different areas of life there are! In the Life Areas Worksheet, Figure B, we have listed some of them. We have purposely put three columns after the list of life areas to help you consider those life areas to which you have a commitment, those which reflect your general situation, or those for which you have or should have goals.

Go down the list. Add other items to it. You are a special person in a special situation. You need to see the whole person, a person made up of all of the different assets of your life.

To be completely a whole person is (1) to understand who you are, where you have come from, what your present commitments are and (2) to have a clear picture of where you believe God wants you to move.

By including in our thinking all our present commitments and our entire present situation, and by not compartmentalizing life into such things as work, family, leisure, etc., we are able to integrate our goals. The better job of integration we do, the more effective we will become as persons.

Ten years from now our life-style may be different than it is at the moment. We should expect it to be. We don't have to remain the same. The possibility of change should always exist. But right now let us consider who we are and where we are, so that we can become all God wants us to be, all God wants us to be as whole persons.

Summing Up

Any discussion about Christian living, especially goal setting and establishing priorities, that deals with only one portion of life is bound to fail. We need to see ourselves as whole persons. Each of us has a different life. Each one of us is made up of a different history, lives in a different situation, has different commitments and obligations, and has different needs and goals. As we seek Christian goals for our life, we need to see *all* of our life and all of its relationships.

Something for You to Do

Go down the Life Areas Worksheet, Figure B. Put a check after each area in which you have a commitment or which bears on your present situation. Now go through these same

LIFE AREAS WORKSHEET

AREAS	COMMITMENTS	SITUATION	GOALS
God			
Spouse			
Children			
Relatives			
Friends			
Business Associates			
Others			
Learning			
Relaxation			
Recreation			
Hobbies			
Physical Well-being			
Emotional Well-being			
Spiritual Well-being			
Occupation			
Employer			
Finances			
Service to God			
Service to the Body			
Service to Humanity			
Educational Achievement			
Technical Achievement			
Social Achievement			
Financial Achievement			
Career Achievement			
Spiritual Achievement			
Acquisition of Things			
Home			
Car			
Clothes			
Parenthood			
Retirement			
Future			

Figure B

areas. In light of your commitments and your present situation, place a check next to each one for which you believe you should set a goal.

What other areas of your life are not listed on this worksheet? Note them and ask yourself the same questions about them.

Something for You to Do with Your Spouse

First carry out the same exercise suggested above, working independently of one another. Then compare your sheets. You will find this an excellent communication device as you note areas where one person thought there was a commitment and the other one did not.

Particularly notice places where you agreed or disagreed on the need for setting goals. This will tell you a great deal about each other and about planning your future together.[2]

Footnotes

1. Psychologists, of course, recognize that many of our conscious and subconscious actions are rooted in our *perception* of our past. This is why it is so often necessary for the counselor to lead a person through a review of his or her past and to make peace with the past so that person can move into the future.

2. If this raises more problems than you can handle, try H. Norman Wright's *Communication: Key to Your Marriage* (Glendale, CA: Regal Books, 1974).

CHAPTER 13

LIVING A STRATEGIC LIFE

Let us assume that you understand who you are in terms of your history, your present situation and your present commitments. You understand that life is a whole and you can't live a compartmentalized life.

How can you fit this all together in a practical sense? How can you select goals which are better, more appropriate for you?

Filling Empty Calendars

Let's pretend for a moment that you are going to plan all of your time for a whole month, every hour of it. No one would actually do things this way, of course, but the exercise of doing so will help us get some handles on some very practical applications. Think ahead to sometime in the future when you have a blank calendar. That might be next month, or it might be twelve months from now.

Now, let us suppose that you are going to fill up the calendar by scheduling first things first. First, time for goals which have the highest priority. This would mean that you would first schedule times for goals that had to do with all of your commitments to Christ. After that, you would put down times that had to do with your commitment to the Body of Christ. Next you would schedule time that had to do with the work of Christ.

Last, you would fill in the rest with time for doing all of the other things that you need to do to get on with this business of living. In all of this you would be trying to see life as a whole, trying to see how each part related to another part.

Why a calendar? Well, if we are dealing with *personal* goals, then we are talking about future events over which we believe we have some control. There is no sense in having a *personal* goal for something which is completely outside of yourself. What you really need to do is *set goals for your time,* for your life is made up of time. Time is life. Life is time.

When we speak of a "full life" or "three score years and ten," we are talking about a time dimension. Your calendar reflects *you.* Who you are and what you are, are best described by what you do and, just as importantly, when you do it.

So, back to our calendar. Let's make a specific date, a time commitment for each of these three levels of commitment. What kind of dates might we make?

Time with God

When are you going to be consciously communing with God through worship, prayer, meditation or reading His Word? "Oh," you may say, "I don't have to write down those dates. Those are just things that I *do.* They are habits that I have." That may be true, but if you don't write down such time commitments on your calendar, how will you keep track of the ones that you have missed? Shouldn't your calendar reflect the most important commitments that you have, the very special ones?

When we break an appointment with another person, either intentionally or unintentionally, we usually immediately think about when we can make it up, reschedule it. But too often we never think to make up time with the Lord!

If you are a member of one of the civic clubs, such as the Rotary, then perhaps you are aware that if you miss a meeting, you must make it up at some other time. If you miss too many meetings, you are automatically dropped from membership. It is assumed that you are not interested! Why can't we apply the same principle to the most important relationship in the world? We read of Jesus: "In the morning, a great while before day, he rose and went out to a lonely place, and there he prayed" (Mark 1:35, RSV). There were all kinds of people who needed His help. There were lepers to be healed, demons to be cast out. There were lessons to be taught, men to be discipled. But when it came to allocating His time, Jesus' first thought appears to be time with His Father.

We need this same type of thinking. If we are "behind" in our times with the Lord, then we need to make dates with Him. Could it be that right now you need to schedule an entire morning or an entire day which would be given to quiet reflecting on His will for your life and what goals He would have you set to be more conformed to His will?

Time with Your Spouse

If time with the Body of Christ is the second level of commitment, who within that Body should have a priority? We believe that the Bible gives a very clear answer: "A man shall leave his father and mother, and shall cleave unto his wife: and they shall be one flesh" (see Gen. 2:24).[1] Is there a date on your calendar with your husband or wife? There need to be times when you are going to be building into each other's life.

A relationship is like a beautiful garden. It will maintain its beauty only as it is cultivated and watered. Because we are living together, it does not follow that we are *growing* together.

Two people can spend a lifetime under the same roof and never really know each other. There need to be programs to strengthen your marriage, goals to make your spouse a more effective person. Whatever else this mysterious "one flesh" means, it certainly means recognition of your need for one another.

Time with Your Family

What next? As you make dates on this imaginary calendar, what other members of the Body claim a high priority? Certainly the rest of your family is high on such a list. Do you have a date with your young son or your teenage daughter? Is it on your calendar or in your appointment book? What? Have you never had the fun of escorting your beautiful daughter to a local restaurant or having your handsome son take you somewhere?

Are family times scheduled and guarded? Or could it be that you are one of those parents who is so "committed to the Lord" that your children view Him as someone who is always stealing the time that was committed to them? Suppose members of your family looked at your datebook right now? Would they see *evidence* that they really are high on your list of priorities?

If you are a single person you need to have time with your brothers and sisters, as well as your parents, if that is possible geographically. They, too, are top priority in Christ's family. "If anyone does not make provision for his relations, and especially for members of his own household, he has denied the faith and is worse than an unbeliever" (1 Tim. 5:8, *NEB*).

Time for You

We may surprise you with our suggestion for your next appointment. We believe that your next priority should be time for *you*. You need to make some dates with yourself!

There need to be times when you are going to have a relief valve from the pressures that always come. Perhaps you can find these through a regular program of recreation, such as bowling or tennis. Or perhaps there needs to be a time when you just do nothing. One of us is an avid golfer while the other likes to sit on the beach and watch the waves and the boats go by. Whatever fits your life-style is what you need here.

Think about your typical calendar and your typical week or month. When it begins to get loaded up with too many evenings out, too much pressure, that is the time to schedule time completely to yourself. And by putting it down on the calendar you can "protect it" from demands which will almost always come. If you are too embarrassed to write "Me" down in your appointment book, just write in "Busy."

Does it work? We sometimes jokingly remark that if someone telephones you with an urgent appeal to come to a very important meeting or address a *very* important audience, and you tell him you have a date with your nine-year-old son, he may continue to try to persuade you. On the other hand, if you tell him that you are sorry, but you have a date with *yourself,* that will probably end the discussion. And he may never call you again!

Is this selfishness or just building up yourself at the expense of others? Shouldn't we spend and be spent? We recognize that there is a tension here. But one of the paradoxes of life is that you are all that you have. When *you* are worn out, you've had it!

We need to say it again: God is much more interested in *you* than in what you have accomplished. Another side of the paradox is that only as you care for the person—yourself—that God has given you are you able to be effective in caring for others.

Time for Fellowship

After time for your wife and family and time for you, start putting down time with your brothers and sisters in Christ. When are you going to be worshiping, praying, studying or fellowshiping with them? When is there going to be time for discipleship? Evangelism

There are at least four different kinds of relationships that might be considered here. First, there is your relationship to the total local Body of Christ, your church. Regardless of your view of ecclesiastical structures, the Bible leaves very little doubt that each Christian should see himself or herself as related to a local fellowship of believers.

Second, there is the possibility of being in a cell group within the church or with members from different local fellowships. Probably the people who need this the most are "professional" Christians. (We just can't seem to find a better phrase.) Too often we become so busy ministering to others that we never permit anyone to minister to us. Whether it is a prayer group, Bible study group, fellowship group, does not matter. What is important is that there is a place within which you can have Christian relationships, a place where you can hear and be heard.[2]

Third, if you are married, there is the possibility of having a relationship to another couple or a number of couples. Here again, we all have a need to relate to others whose situations are similar to ours, to be able to discuss our Christian experience and our understanding of God's Word within the context of our marriage.

Fourth is the vital need to have a one-to-one relationship with another Christian, man-to-man or woman-to-woman. Paul had Timothy; David had Jonathan. There needs to be someone on whom you can call when you are in a time of need or a time of rejoicing. Such deep relationships are not easily obtained. The risk of rejection or failure is high. But the value of knowing and being known cannot be overestimated.

Can we say a special word to pastors here? Pastor, you above all people cannot go it alone. The idea that the pastor and his wife cannot afford to have close friendships in a congregation is a myth. You can't afford *not* to have them.

Unplanned Time for Others

We are still filling in that empty calendar. What next? What about time for other people, *unplanned* time when you are going to be available for their goals?

If you devote all of your schedule to *your* programs, you will not only be unable to take unexpected opportunities to help others, but you will be continually pushed by outside demands you cannot meet. If every night of the week is full with meetings and outside engagements, if every day's calendar is so tight there is no room for give, then pressures can become almost unbearable.

Consider putting down "Time for Others" in blocks on your calendar. Leave at least two evenings a week free. Perhaps you need to have some rule that says you will only fill up those empty lines with dates with people who call today or the day before. Whatever your system may be, remember that others need you too. Their schedule will not always fit yours.

Time for Personal Planning

Last, under this area of time with the Body, we would like to suggest that you write down *time to do personal planning.* You might wonder what this has to do with your relationships to others. It has many implications.

Planning has to do with the way you hope to do things in the future, and that certainly involves not only you, but all the people in your life. If you don't put on your calendar times to plan, there is a good possibility that you never will take time to plan.

Perhaps you need a short time daily to think about the day's plans, and a longer time weekly to think about the week ahead. Have at least one day a year when you contemplate how you will spend the coming year. Only in this way can you begin to *manage* your life in a way which will honor God, to live life with a purpose.

Pray over your plans. Planning and prayers should be

intimately entwined. Plans too are statements of faith. When we bring our plans before the Lord, we should be saying in effect, "Lord, this is what I believe you want me to do, this is the way I intend to carry it out, trusting that I am in your will and believing that if this is not the approach that I am to take, you will reveal that to me also."

Time for the "Work"

We are speaking here specifically about Christian work, that which is done purposefully for the Kingdom. For the Christian "professional," this may be the same thing as his livelihood. For the "layman," it is intended to mean all of the things that one is called upon to do in his role as a Christian. This would mean that if you were continuing to fill out your calendar, you would begin to schedule such things as Sunday School, attending a board meeting, serving on the committee of a Christian organization. Evangelism etc.

Scheduling for Freedom

By now you may have begun to appreciate that thinking about scheduling your time in this way can be a very *freeing* concept. When most people think about schedules and calendars, they think of rigid deadlines and constraining structures. They fear that by "over-scheduling" they will give up all of their ability to move at the impulse of the Spirit.

What we are suggesting here is something quite different. As we picture it, schedules and appointments are fences which we build around our time to give us freedom. The area within the fence is kept broad enough so that there is room to move around. Some of the fenced-off areas are even empty!

So we say, "Fill up the calendar!" But don't fill it up with commitments. Leave in those empty spaces and protect them. Of course, this is no guarantee that the future will fall in place as you schedule it. Quite often a herd of buffalo will go roaring through your life, completely destroying all of your best laid plans. But at least you will know from the broken fences that they have been there, and you can set about rebuilding—rescheduling according to your Christian value system.

It's a Process

All of this must be seen as a *process,* a repetitive process: goals, priorities, planning, living. There will be many interrelationships. One goal may cover a number of areas. One time block may cover a number of goals. There will be conflicts between goals as they struggle for our time. One may cancel out another.

We can lay out the three broad levels of priorities and attempt to work within these. They can become a framework within which we can manage our life in a God-honoring way. But tomorrow is in the Lord's hands. The best way to walk within His good will for us is to continue to review our current goals in light of these levels of commitment.

Summing Up

When we begin to select goals for our life we must see them as goals for a *whole* person. Our life is made up of our history, our present situation, our commitments and our goals. We need to take the first three into account as we plan for the last.

As we begin to select goals in the light of the three levels of commitment—commitment to God and Christ, commitment to the Body of Christ, and commitment to the work of Christ, there are some very specific areas which should be considered. One way to keep the areas in proper perspective is to imagine that we are making up a schedule for each one. Within such a schedule we should think about goals for time with God, time for our family, and for ourselves, time for other members of the Body of Christ, unplanned time for others' goals, time to plan and time for the work of Christ.

By scheduling in time for the others and unplanned time, we can use our schedule to give us *more* freedom. We can build fences around pieces of our life—our time—that will give us freedom to move. All of this is a process. We set goals, establish priorities, do our planning and then begin to live out our plans. This, in turn, will immediately force us back to reconsidering our goals and our priorities.

Remember the definition of a goal: a future event which is accomplishable and measurable. Make sure that as you write your goals they meet those two criteria. Look at the examples we have given you and then try writing some of your own. It will help to look again at the Life Areas Worksheet in Chapter 12, Figure B. In light of this chapter are there areas here for which you should have specific goals?

Something for You to Do

In Figure A we have given you another example of how to fill in a goal worksheet. One way to better understand what we are trying to say in this chapter is to attempt to write a goal for each of the seven areas we have described.

Something to Do with Your Spouse

Review your schedules, calendars or appointment books together for the past month and the forthcoming month. How much of what you are doing are you doing together? Is any part of what you are doing also part of some *family* goals? Where do you need to schedule family times and dates with each other?

Footnotes

1. See also Matthew 19:5; Mark 10:7; 1 Corinthians 6:16 and Ephesians 5:31.
2. If you're having difficulty in making a group work, an excellent book on group dynamics and how an effective group works is *Joining Together* by David W. Johnson and Frank P. Johnson (Englewood Cliffs, NJ: Prentice-Hall, 1975). A workbook on group theory and group decision making, group goal setting, group leadership, communication within groups and group problem solving, *Joining Together* contains a number of skill training exercises. It is a good book for anyone involved in leading a group within an organization or in a non-organizational setup.

GOALS WORKSHEET

What do I want to happen? (Accomplishment)	How will I know it happened? (Measurement) (Date)	Hours/Week Needed
Time with God *Spend 30 minutes a day in a devotional study of book of Matthew, starting Sept. 1 until complete.*		3½
Time with my family *Make a weekly date with wife and review my weekly calendar with her on Saturday morning in advance, starting Sept. 4.*		3
Time for me *Work out one hour per week at gym by setting time on calendar and having wife check up on me.*		2
Time with the Body (planned) *Invite Bill Rogers and Jerry Hunt to have a weekly breakfast sharing time starting Oct. 1.*		2
Time for others (unplanned) *Keep 2 hours free each day to help others toward their goal by setting time on calendar starting next week.*		10
Time to plan *Spend 20 minutes between 8–9 a.m. daily to consider and organize my tasks and direction.*		2
Time for the work of Christ *Teach Sunday School, 5th grade, during the next quarter.*		5–10

Figure A

PART VI CLOSING THE CIRCLE

14 How to Set Goals for Your Life
15 Designing a New Life
16 Toward More Effective Living
17 Time Is Life
18 You Have a Strategy for Living

CHAPTER 14

HOW TO SET GOALS
FOR YOUR LIFE

We have discussed goals and their importance. We have tried to relate priorities to the Christian life. We have shown you some ways to do some personal planning. We have emphasized the need to deal with life as a whole. We have used the example of filling in a calendar to indicate how all of this might relate to everyday living.

Now the circle begins to close. Now we are ready to discuss a total program for your life. We are ready to discuss how to set goals for life.

If you are like many people, you feel "over-committed." You have a terrible sense of your life being somehow controlled by forces that are outside of you. You want God to be at the center of your life, but so many things seem to get in the way. You have family commitments. You have commitments to your church. You have responsibilities to mothers and fathers, sisters and brothers, sons and daughters. Your employer or employees put demands upon your time and expect you to work toward *their* goals. And when you try to imagine how you can move out of the situation that you are in, it just doesn't seem possible. The world is just too complex.

There are a number of responses to such feelings. First, we can just drop out. "These are the end times. The Lord will be coming soon. There is no sense in my worrying about the future. I'll just take whatever comes." Hezekiah had a similar view when he was happy over the fact that the calamity was not going to happen in his day, "For he thought, 'Why not, if there will be peace and security in my days?' " (2 Kings 20:19, *RSV*).

Or we can adopt a view of passive optimism and hope that somehow the stream of life will flow into better channels in the days ahead. In our "upwardly mobile" society, many Americans find this the easiest route to go. "After all," we reason, "haven't we always found a solution to the world's problems? My company will probably take care of me, or I (or my husband) will probably get a better job someday."

Part of our difficulty in facing such a complex world is that we usually overestimate what we can do in one year and underestimate what we can do in five or ten. If you stop and think for a moment, don't you believe that you could do or be almost anything if you were given ten years to do it? Of course, if you are already 45, you probably will never be a tackle in the National Football League or win a Miss America contest. But you could be a doctor; you could be a writer; you could be active in political life.

The secret is to set goals far enough into the future so that you are unencumbered by the present. We need to dream great dreams, to imagine what could be and then to work our way back into the present, into reality.

Here's How to Go About It

Set aside some time, at least an hour, in the near future, a time when you can be by yourself and away from any interruptions. Pick a place that is comfortable for you, a place that you associate with freedom and pleasant thoughts. Take along a pad and pencil so you can jot down some of your thoughts.

Now fantasize in prayer. Imagine what you would really *like* to be doing 5 or 10 or 15 years from now. Get into a mental helicopter and fly over your dream world. Look down. What are you doing? Where are you living? Who are your friends? Are you married? Do you have children? What is your occupation? What is happening in your daily life? What are your hobbies? What are you *enjoying?* Perhaps you always wanted to learn to fly. Was there a book that you wanted to write someday? Did you really want to be a preacher or a more effective parent? What dreams do you have for your wife, your husband or your children? What are they doing in this scene that you're viewing from your mental helicopter?

As you start making this kind of mental helicopter flight, you may have a little difficulty. You might wonder, for example, if what you *should* be doing and what you *would like* to do are supposed to be the same. Perhaps you have had training or heard preaching that gives you the sneaking suspicion that God really doesn't want you to like what you're doing. This is a most unhappy view of the Almighty! Remember that God has promised to give us the *desires* of our hearts! (see Ps. 37:4). The trials and temptations of life will always be there, but our God is a God who is *for* us!

Another problem that you may encounter on your mental helicopter journey is getting off the ground. Perhaps fantasizing about 10 or 15 years from now is a bit more than you can grasp at first. In his book, *How to Get Control of Your Time and Your Life,*[1] Alan Lakein suggests two questions that might help trigger your thinking. The first is, "If I knew I would be dead at the end of the next six months, how would I live until then?" The second is, "How would I like to spend the next three years?" Try them. They are good starters that can help you "take off."

Include your far-out wishes and fantasies in your goal dreaming. Write down whatever comes to your mind. This could seem silly, even embarrassing, but if you think those thoughts, why not write them down where you can look at them? (God knows all about them anyway.) Bob Pierce, the founder and former president of World Vision International, a man who has meant much to both of us, used to caution us to *leave God room* in our planning. As Christians, we have a right to believe God can do great things with us.

While you are praying and dreaming, make a few notes, notes about this life that you are living. From these notes write down a Life Goal statement. You will no doubt have to come back and refine this as you go through the process, but note it now. Perhaps it can only be stated as a purpose that needs to be supported by a number of goals. It might be a good idea to go back and review Chapter 5, which defines the difference between goals and purposes. In addition, look again at Chapter 6, which discusses seven simple steps to setting goals. We are going to use those seven steps again right here to help you fantasize about your goals for 10 to 15 years from now.

For an example of how the seven steps could be used to make a "Life Goals Worksheet," let's take the hypothetical case of Frank, a 38-year-old insurance salesman with a congenial wife named Marge. Frank and Marge are very active in their church and have often talked and dreamed about serving on the mission field in some way. So, in order to make their dreams come true, Frank sat down and went through the seven steps for setting goals (see Fig. A).

Now that you have the idea from Frank's Life Goals Worksheet, try going through the seven steps yourself. If you have been doing any jotting on your note pad while on that mental helicopter flight, you should already have some of the steps completed.

LIFE GOALS WORKSHEET

Done by Frank, a would-be missionary

STEP 1: *Understand your purpose in life.* Note all the different purposes you can think of.

To serve the church in an underdeveloped country for at least two years.

STEP 2: *Picture the situation.* Imagine the situation not as it is now, but how it would be like if you realized your life purpose.

Kids grown up. Marge free to go. Adequate cultural understanding. Enough money available. I'm probably 50.

STEP 3: *State your long-range goals.* What measurable and accomplishable events would have to happen in order for that purpose to be realized?

1. Saved $20,000 in next 20 years.
2. Language of country learned and culture understood by end of 20 years.
3. Kids education completed and paid for in next 20 years.

STEP 4: *State your immediate goals.* What are the things you have to work on right now if you're going to move toward your ultimate purpose?

1. Set up $1,000/year savings plan during next month.
2. Reduce life-style to give adequate extra finances by end of this year.
3. Work out long-range plan with Marge and kids in next six months.

STEP 5: *Act.* Pick out one of those goals and decide what you can do right now, today, or at the latest, tomorrow.

Open up savings account tomorrow

STEP 6: *Act as if . . .* Note ways you might be acting if you were really moving toward this goal.

Change life-style.

STEP 7: *Keep praying.* Prayerfully review what you have written. Is this God's best plan for you? Modify it. Change it. Now restate your life goals.

Ask God for wisdom.

Figure A

Step 1—Understand your purpose. You have probably already done that. You have a general picture of what it is you would like to become, what it is you would like to be, what it is you would like to accomplish. You have written down the statement about how the world is going to be different because you were a part of it.

Step 2—Picture the situation. You have probably done that too. You have flown around in your mental helicopter and decided where you would like to be, what you would like to be doing, and so forth.

Step 3—State some long-range goals. Still thinking *backward* from the future to the present, *what steps might you have to take to realize your goals for five years from now?* For instance, if you would like to be practicing medicine 15 years from now, perhaps you should have nearly completed medical school 5 years from now. Or, if you pictured yourself in a different profession 15 years from now, 5 years from now you probably should be trained for that. Again, if you would like to be working somewhere overseas, perhaps 5 years from now you should have arranged your family life so this is possible and saved a given amount of money.

Maybe right now you are the mother of three small children. All of your life is centered around them. But what will it be like 15 years from now? Perhaps you should be planning to enroll in an evening course one night a week, a course that will lead you to a new life-style after your children are grown.

Write down some of these specific things you would have to do and then note with each one of them the steps you would have to take in order to accomplish them. Ask yourself the question, "What would have to happen before this could happen?" Go back now and look at your Life Goals statement. Does it need to be refined at this point? Can you get it nailed down to more specifics? Now write down your Life Goals statement on a 3x5 card.

Step 4—State your immediate goals. You are almost back to

the present with the picture of the future you have sketched out. *What steps do you have to take right now?* Remember, *no one can make decisions about the future.* All decisions are about the present. But what we *can* do is make decisions now which will permit us to do things in the future. Set specific goals for things you can do one month from now or two months from now. Write these down, also perhaps on a 3x5 card, or on some piece of paper that you can carry along with your Life Goals statement.

If you are married, share your immediate goals with your spouse. Perhaps you should share them with no one else because others may just discourage you from believing you can accomplish what you have set out to do. But your husband or wife is a part of you. You are "one flesh."[2] And this highest of all human commitments needs to be built upon shared goals. To build your own goals, it is necessary to come to some conclusion about shared goals.

It goes without saying that if you are going to go through this process, it will be most effective if your husband or wife goes through it independently at the same time. You may be surprised at the divergence in the conclusions to which you come, but as we will note later, it will certainly strengthen communication within your marriage!

Step 5—Act. Pick out one of the goals and start moving toward it.

Step 6—Act as if . . . you are already on the way toward your goals. This is both good psychology and good Christianity. What we believe and what we think are important. But much more important is what we *do.* For what we do is living demonstration of what we actually believe. It is true that the way we think controls our actions. It is equally true that the way we act eventually will control our thinking.

Step 7—Keep praying. Review those short-range goals regularly. Pray them in. These are *statements of faith* about what you believe God wants you to do in the coming days. You are saying to God, "Lord, this is what I intend to do, because I believe this is going to lead me to be the kind of a person you want me to be or do that which you want me to do. If you have other plans, reveal those to me."

Suppose It Doesn't Work?

Let's suppose you have tried a mental helicopter flight, you have studied the sample of Frank, the would-be missionary, and you have tried to go through the seven steps. But you are still having trouble. Perhaps you feel that you just cannot imagine the kind of a future you would like. This might be because you are just starting out in life or because you are nearing its conclusion. Or perhaps you feel that you just don't know what the opportunities are.

Here's another approach that can help: Make a list of all the things you *like to do.* Start by making a list of the things you have done in the past six months that you really like to do. Then make a list of things you have done in the last week that you really like to do. If you are doing things like these all of the time, five years from now, what kind of a profession might you be in, or what might your relationships be to others, or where might you be living?[3] In one sense, that's "all there is to it." If you start the practice of setting long-range goals and "act as if," you are on the way to accomplishing them. You can well bring about a major revolution in your life.

In his book, *The Age of Discontinuity,*[4] Peter Drucker points out that if you graduate from college this year, you will have to retrain two more times before you retire. That's why we believe you need a *strategy* for living. There are no "final" answers to life, only godly beginnings.

It's a Process

Setting goals for life is *not* a one-time exercise. The world keeps changing. We keep changing. The situations around us keep changing. The things we imagined would happen or would not happen will surprise us. We need to keep on pressing on. If you go through this same exercise six months or one year from now, you may have a new understanding of where you should be somewhere in the future. The important thing about the process is that it gives us a *sense of direction* and thus gives us a purpose. This sense of direction, this perception of knowing what we believe we should do and what we should not do, helps us gain greater control over our lives. Now we can see ourselves in the process of *becoming* and as we have a better picture of where we are going, so we are better able to relate to others.

Goals, priorities, planning, living—that's the process. Our priorities will determine how we value our life and our planning will determine whether we accomplish our goals.

Everyone Should Do It

Perhaps you are thinking that this is a good exercise for the husband or the head of the household and that the rest of the family should fit into his goals and plans. This is neither biblical nor practical. Ephesians 5:21 tells us to submit to one another. It shows the husband's "submission" as being on an order of magnitude so great that it can only be compared to the love that Christ has for His Church (see Eph. 5:25).

An integral part of building one another up is to have an understanding of one another's goals and purposes. Try it yourself. Encourage your spouse to do the same thing. Work with your pre-teens toward thinking through what their lives are going to be like.[5] Remember we are *the Body* of Christ, and the Body works together only when each member is performing his special assignment.

Summing Up

The secret to escaping those feelings of being trapped and over-committed is to set your goals far enough in the future so that you are unencumbered by the present. Let yourself go and

141

dream great dreams. Make a mental helicopter flight and look down to see how you would like to be living 5, 10, 15 years from now.

Use the seven steps for goal setting (review Chapter 5) to work out a "Life Goals Worksheet." Don't get bogged down if it does not come easily. Try the various suggestions in this chapter to practice setting long-range goals and "act as if" you are on the way to accomplishing them.

Remember that setting goals for life is a *continual* process. As circumstances change, your goals may change, but as you go through the process of goal setting from time to time, you have a sense of direction for life—a strategy for living.

Something for You to Do

If you haven't already tried the process described in this chapter, make a date with yourself right now. Use the sample worksheet for Frank (Fig. A) and make your own "Life Goals Worksheet," using the seven steps for goal setting.

Something to Do with Your Spouse

We have already mentioned the need for husband and wife to work together in goal setting. Here is one more idea: Make a list of your purposes in life and a separate list of the goals that you believe might lead to those purposes. Now make a list of what you believe are your *spouse's* purposes in life and goals that she or he might set to reach those purposes. Exchange your lists and then analyze them together to see where you have a difference of perception and where you need to work together toward a family set of purposes and goals.

Something for You to Do with Others

In a group of three to six people, give each person a large sheet of newsprint and a felt-tip pen or crayon. Ask each person to list things he or she has done during the past week or month that were enjoyable, gratifying or pleasant.

Ask each person to print in fairly large letters and then put his list up where everyone can see it. (You may want to have some masking tape handy for attaching the lists to the wall.)

Then have the group spend five minutes on each person's list. Go around the circle and let everyone comment on the person being evaluated. What kind of person do they perceive that person to be on the basis of his or her likes or preferences? You will discover that this is an affirming experience and will help the individual to gain some insight into his gifts and abilities.

Footnotes

1. Alan Lakein, *How to Get Control of Your Time and Your Life* (New York: Peter H. Wyden, 1973).
2. See Genesis 2:24; Matthew 19:5; Mark 10:7; 1 Corinthians 6:16 and Ephesians 5:31.
3. An excellent book to help you decide upon and land the job you want is Richard N. Bolles' *What Color Is Your Parachute?* (New York: Crown, 1973).
4. Peter Drucker, *The Age of Discontinuity* (New York: Harper and Row, 1969).
5. In his book, *Hide or Seek* (Old Tappan, NJ: Fleming H. Revell, 1974), James Dobson suggests that just before your child becomes a teenager, one parent should spend a day away with him or her and discuss what the future will be like. Dobson encourages us to write down for our child a description of that future, so that when he is in the middle of teenage turmoil, he can read it over and remember that Dad or Mom said it would be like that, but it *will* get better. The goal is to live through it!

CHAPTER 15

DESIGNING A NEW LIFE

All right, let us suppose you have gone through the life goal-setting exercises described in the last chapter. You now have a nice list of goals you would enjoy pursuing. You may feel that you are now ready to start planning to meet those goals. Before you move on, however, it's a good idea to evaluate your goals to be sure they (1) are practical and realistic, (2) take into account your present life-style.

To put it another way, before deciding where you intend to go, it's a good idea to decide where you are now. What we suggest in this chapter will take time. If you are ready to go through all the steps, it will be time well spent. But if you aren't quite ready, don't get bogged down. You don't have to do everything suggested here before finishing the book. Read the chapter and note how all the steps are illustrated in the sample case study. You can come back later, if necessary, and try these steps for yourself.

Things Are as They Are

It is a trite, but very true statement: Things are as they are. To put it another way, *you* are as you are now. You cannot do much about your past history, but you can understand your present commitments and your present situation. This understanding will help you discover whether your goals are realistic and whether you have included among them all of the things you need to do.

Remember how we discussed in Chapter 12 that we needed to live *all* of life? We need to see ourselves as whole people. We used the diagram (Fig. A) to indicate each one of us is made up of his history, his present situation, his commitments and his goals.

How can you discover if your goals match up with your present situation? If you use the six steps described in this chapter you will have a better view of where you are going and you will learn a great deal about yourself as well.

To evaluate your goals, go through these six steps:

1. Analyze your present commitments.
2. See how you perceive you are spending your time.
3. Take an actual inventory of how you spend your time daily.
4. Look at your calendar of appointments (if you keep one).
5. Compare your goals against your present commitments, your perception of how you spend your time, your time inventory and your appointment calendar.
6. Restate your list of goals as needed.

To help you see how all this works, we have given you the example of Bill, a 30-year-old engineer with a wife and two small children. We have a list of goals for Bill (see Fig. A) and

146

BILL'S GOALS

1. To spend an average of one half hour each day in personal prayer and Bible study.

2. To save $10,000 during the next four years for the children's education.

3. To receive a Master of Engineering degree two years from next June.

4. To spend one hour a week alone with each of the children.

5. To establish an in-depth fellowship group with four other couples by May 11.

6. To move from my present job into a similar job in the field of energy conservation by January 1.

7. Have two day vacation alone with Betty by the end of next month.

8. To serve the church in an underdeveloped country for a period of at least two years when I am between the ages of 50 and 55.

9. To increase our family giving to 20% of our gross income by the end of next year.

Figure A

we have also worked out some simple forms that take him through the six steps outlined above.

As you go through Bill's example, you can (if you wish) evaluate your own set of goals to see if they are practical and realistic. But remember, if you are not quite ready to do all these exercises, don't let that stop you. Finish the chapter and come back to these six steps when you are ready, perhaps even after finishing the book.

Present Commitments

The first step is to analyze your present commitments—jobs, assignments, committee responsibilities, bills, debts, etc., etc. In Figure B we've filled out the form as Bill might have done. Note that the form includes personal and family commitments. This is important, because Bill is part of a family (and you probably are, too).

Make your own form and use Bill's example to list as many of your own commitments as you can. These might include family, job, finances, hobbies, friends, causes to which you are committed—anything for which and to which you believe you have a commitment. If you would like a little help to prime the pump on listing commitments, why not look again at the Life Areas Worksheet in Chapter 12.

After each commitment listed, indicate whether it is personal—yours alone—or whether it is jointly shared by you and other members of your family. A personal commitment might be a commitment to your wife, or, on a much smaller scale your agreement to serve on a church committee. A shared commitment might be one which you and your wife or family have toward your local church or, at a more mundane level, the promissory note you both signed when you borrowed money from the bank to pay for the family car.

Why look at our commitments? For one thing, there are some that cannot change. There are certain givens, such as your commitment to your husband or wife, that cannot be revoked.

BILL'S COMMITMENTS

COMMITMENT	PERSONAL	FAMILY
My wife, Betty	X	
Trinity Church		X
$1,000 loan to United Bank	X	
Complete the Alpha Project by June 1	X	
neighborhood collection for Heart Fund next month	X	
Weekly breakfast with Bill Jones	X	
Funds for kids' education		X
monthly car payment of $92.		X
Board of Orange Street Mission	X	
Taking Billy to the Park each week	X	
Reading and praying with Nancy before bed nightly.	X	
Tennis club membership and weekly matches	X	

Figure B

On the other hand, there are many commitments which eventually can be discharged so that we can move on to new things. Winston Churchill is quoted as saying, "It's not enough that we do our best; sometimes we have to do what's required."

An excellent way of gaining some insight is to have another member of your family (your spouse, if you are married) fill out a sheet *for you.* Have them list those things *they* believe you are committed to. If you are married, we suggest that you also might want to have your spouse fill out the same kind of sheet for himself or herself so that you can review your commitments together.

Warning: This can lead to some surprising and sometimes disturbing insights. You may discover that you are committed to quite different things or you may discover that what you thought was a family commitment was really one to which only *you* are committed.

How Are You Spending Your Time?

The next step is to perceive how you are spending your time. In Figure C you can see how Bill did it. Use the example to make an evaluation of your own time and how you are spending it. List anything that comes to mind—at home, with your business, with your family, your spiritual life—anything at all.

As you move along, or after you have completed the list, evaluate each item. What do you think about this particular time investment? Do you believe that for the area you have listed you are spending too *little* time, just the right amount of time, or too *much* time?

What Does Your Time Inventory Say?

Next comes the most difficult assignment of all, one which is wisely used in many areas of organizational life, but one which is hard to carry out. We suggest that for an entire week you keep track of everything you do in fifteen-minute increments

BILL'S PERCEPTION OF HIS TIME

HOW AM I SPENDING MY TIME? Note anything that comes to mind: home, business, family, spiritual life, etc.	How Much Do I Spend?		
	Too Little	Just Right	Too Much
Business meetings			X
Church Board			X
Personal devotions	X		
Time with Betty	X		
Work interruption			X
Driving to work			X
Watching TV			X
Woodworking hobby	X		
Playing with kids	X		
Prayer group	X		
Professional education	X		
Reading the newspaper		X	
Sleeping		X	
Eating	X		
Leisure	X		
Planning	X		

Figure C

BILL'S DAILY TIME INVENTORY

	MONDAY	TUESDAY	WEDNESDAY
7:00	Awoke + dressed		
7:30	Breakfast, Read together		
8:00	Drive to office		
8:30	Look over mail sort for reply		
9:00	worked on Johnson project		
9:30	Read technical magazines		
10:00	Called Johnson coffee break		
10:30	Johnson project		
11:00			
11:30	↓		
12:00	Lunch with Abe		
12:30			
1:00	↓		
1:30	talked to secretary		
2:00	phone calls Talked to Ros. B		
2:30	↓		
3:00	Worked on Johnson coffee break		
3:30	Johnson project		
4:00	answered mail		
4:30	Talked to Boss		
5:00	Drove home		
5:30	Read newspaper		
6:00	Had dinner		
6:30	Read newspaper		
7:00	Drove to meeting Board meeting		
7:30			
8:00			
8:30	↓		
9:00	Drove Home		
9:30			
10:00	Talked to wife Went to sleep		

Figure D

from the time you wake up until you go to bed. In order to carry out such an assignment, you may need help from your family or fellow workers. See Figure D for a one-day sample of how Bill kept a time inventory for a week. Then make up your own form with enough spaces for a week and make a real effort to fill it in every day.

Why is doing this so difficult? First, very few of us think about our time this closely. We are rather used to having one hour flow into the next, moving from one appointment to another, letting outside circumstances dictate our pace. What seems like a simple idea will, in practice, prove to be quite a chore. But for many years those who have been concerned with helping people manage their lives and manage their tasks have recognized that this kind of a time inventory is the very best way to discover what you really are doing.

When you have finished the week, you probably won't believe the results. "I just couldn't have spent that much time doing *that!*" you may decide. Both of us go through this exercise about once a year. That's about all we can stand, for even with the best intentions none of us do what we think we will do. So all the more reason to try it once and see for yourself. But don't be discouraged. Remember the baseball player who feels success when he hits four times out of ten at bat.

Look at Your Appointments

The last step is to take a close look at your appointment book or calendar for the past month. Figure E shows you one week of Bill's. If you don't have a regular appointment book or calendar, reconstruct the past month as best you can.

Comparing Goals to Practice

Review your list of goals and make sure each one is numbered as in Bill's sample in Figure A. The numbers do not signify any special priority system; they are simply a way of identifying each goal.

153

One Week from Bill's Appointment Book

Monday

12:15 Lunch with abe

7:30 Church Board

Tuesday

7:30 Breakfast with Sam

Wednesday

12:30 Lunch with Betty

7:00 Choir Practice

Thursday

8:30 Project Presentation to department head.

8:00 Bible Study Group

Friday

6:30 Dinner with Rogers

Saturday

9:00 Little League Practice

8:00 "Date with Betty"

Sunday

1:30 Platt's for dinner

Figure E

Now comes the moment of truth! Review each of the four sheets you have completed: time commitments, perception of how time is spent, daily time inventory and appointment book. Next to any entry on each sheet put an identification number of any goal that you feel might be associated with that entry. To see how Bill, our hypothetical engineer, did it, see Figures F to I. Note the several things Bill did that were not associated with his goals. Then try the same exercise yourself. You will probably discover that your batting average just about matches Bill's.

Analyzing the Results

Go back over your worksheets again. Look at the items that apparently have nothing to do with your goals. Why did you do those things that were not associated with your goals? Which were just time wasters? Why were they time wasters? What could you have done about them? Could they have been eliminated? Could they have been delegated to someone else who could have done them just as well? Or does there begin to emerge from all of this some hidden goals, ones which you really have had all along and want to continue to keep?

Look over the things on which you feel you spent too much time. Were they things you wanted to do or things somebody else wanted you to do? Review the things on which you spent too little time. Again, were they things you wanted to do or things others wanted you to do?

What do the answers to these questions tell you about what is directing your life? Again we suggest that you may want to do this with a member of your family or your spouse by having them fill out their perception of how *you* are spending your time. This will give you an idea of how others perceive you.

Rebuild Your Goals

In light of this analysis, decide which goals now seem less important, which should be eliminated and what new ones

BILL'S NEW COMMITMENTS

COMMITMENT	PERSONAL	FAMILY
① my wife, Betty	X	
⑤ Trinity Church		X
② $1,000 loan to United Bank	X	
Complete the Alpha Project by June 1	X	
neighborhood collection for Heart Fund next month	X	
Weekly breakfast with Bill Jones	X	
② Funds for kids' education		X
monthly car payment of $92.		X
Board of Orange Street Mission	X	
④ Taking Billy to the Park each week	X	
④ Reading and praying with Nancy before bed nightly.	X	
Tennis club membership and weekly matches	X	

Figure F

BILL'S PERCEPTION OF HIS TIME

HOW AM I SPENDING MY TIME? Note anything that comes to mind: home, business, family, spiritual life, etc.	How Much Do I Spend?		
	Too Little	Just Right	Too Much
Business meetings			X
Church Board			X
① Personal devotions	X		
⑦ Time with Betty	X		
Work interruption			X
Driving to work			X
Watching TV			X
Woodworking hobby	X		
Playing with kids	X		
⑤ Prayer group	X		
⑧ Professional education	X		
Reading the newspaper		X	
Sleeping		X	
Eating	X		
Leisure	X		
Planning	X		

Figure G

BILL'S DAILY TIME INVENTORY

		MONDAY	TUESDAY	WEDNESDAY
	7:00	Awoke & dressed		
	7:30	Breakfast Read together		
	8:00	Drive to office		
	8:30	Look over mail sort for reply		
	9:00	worked on Johnson project		
	9:30	Read technical magazines		
	10:00	Called Johnson coffee break		
	10:30	Johnson project		
	11:00			
	11:30	↓		
	12:00	Lunch with Abe		
	12:30	⑤		
	1:00	↓		
	1:30	talked to secretary		
	2:00	phone calls Talked to Ros B		
	2:30	↓		
	3:00	Worked on Johnson coffee break		
	3:30	Johnson project		
	4:00	answered mail ↓		
	4:30	Talked to Boss		
	5:00	Drove home		
	5:30	Read newspaper		
	6:00	Had dinner		
	6:30	Read newspaper		
	7:00	Drove to meeting Board meeting		
	7:30			
	8:00			
	8:30	↓		
	9:00	Drove Home		
	9:30			
	10:00	Talked to wife Went to sleep		

Figure H

BILL'S APPOINTMENT BOOK

Monday	Friday
12:15 Lunch with ⑤ abe 7:30 Church Board	6:30 Dinner with Rogers
Tuesday	**Saturday**
7:30 Breakfast with Sam ⑤	9:00 Little League Practice 8:00 "Date with Betty"
Wednesday	**Sunday**
12:30 Lunch with Betty 7:00 Choir Practice	1:30 Platt's for dinner
Thursday	
8:30 Project Presentation to department head. 8:00 Bible Study Group	

Figure I

BILL'S REVISED GOALS

1. To spend an average of one half hour each day in personal prayer and Bible study.

2. To save $10,000 during the next four years for the children's education.

3. To receive a Master of Engineering degree two years from next June.

4. To spend one hour a week alone with each of the children.

5. To establish an in-depth fellowship group with four other couples by May 11.

6. ~~To move from my present job into a similar job in the field of energy conservation by January 1.~~

7. Have two day vacation alone with Betty by the end of next month.

8. To serve the church in an underdeveloped country for a period of at least two years when I am between the ages of 50 and 55.

9. To increase our family giving to 20% of our gross income by the end of next year.

10. To train effective replacement for church by December 31.

Figure J

should be added. It could very well be that from this you will see quite a different set of priorities than the ones you thought you had. See Figure J for how Bill revised his goals in light of his analysis.

As we said at the beginning of this chapter, going through these steps takes time and effort, but it does pay off because it helps you face reality. On one hand you have your goals, your description of the way you would like things to be. On the other hand, you now have a description of *how things really are.* Your situation is very much like the one we talked about under "Planning." You have a NOW and a THEN (see Fig. K).

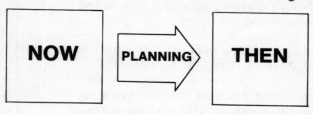

Figure K

But you also have the tools to reach those goals (review especially the section on planning, Chapters 10, 11). It takes work, but doesn't every worthwhile task? Don't be discouraged. Rome wasn't built in a day; neither is a life.

It's a Process

We cannot overemphasize this fact. "Goals, priorities and planning" are the framework within which to think about your life and to manage it more effectively and in a more God-honoring way. Set aside a week during each year in which you will take another inventory, make another assessment of how you are spending your time—managing your life—against the goals that you last set.

Expect your goals to change, because you will change. Situations will change. God will reveal new things to you.

DESIGNING A NEW LIFE	I WILL DO BY THIS DATE	DONE BY
1. I will spend four hours alone thinking about what goals I desire for my life and writing down eight short-range goals and eight long-range goals.		
2. I will spend one half hour listing all of the things to which I and/or my family are committed.		
3. I will spend 15 minutes listing the different ways I am presently spending my time and my own evaluation of them.		
4. I will complete one week of keeping track of all that I do in 15 minute increments.		
5. I will spend one half hour to review my calendar or datebook for the past month.		
6. I will spend two hours comparing my desired goals to the way I'm actually spending my life and against my present commitments.		
7. I will analyze the differences between the way I'm spending my time and my present commitments to the way I would like to spend my time.		
8. I will review my life goals in light of this analysis and write new life goals.		
9. I will make a commitment to the Lord, myself, my spouse and my closest friend to take action.		
10. I will take the first step toward my life goal plan.		

Figure L

"Forgetting what lies behind . . . press on" (Phil. 3:13,14, *RSV*).

Summing Up

Before moving on to plans for reaching your goals, you need first to compare your goals (ideal) with your present situation (actual). One way of doing this is to evaluate your present commitments, evaluate how you perceive you are spending your time, make an inventory of how you are actually spending your time and evaluate your calendar or appointment book. When you match your ideal goals with the results of these four evaluation steps, you will get a "things-as-they-are" overview of your situation. You can then use this comparison to rethink and reshape your initial goals.

It's a process. We have to continually set our goals, review our priorities, make our plans and then start living, recognizing that as we do, we have new information, new insight as to how to live our lives.

If you followed the process outlined in this chapter, you've done enough already. If you haven't, why don't you complete the schedule (Fig. L) on page 163 and use this as a planning guide to get under way. Do it now!

Something to Do with Your Spouse

After completing an analysis of how you spend your own time, try analyzing how you see your spouse's schedule. What is your perception of how he or she is spending his or her time? Then read each other's evaluation and use this as a basis for establishing new family goals.

CHAPTER 16

TOWARD MORE EFFECTIVE LIVING

There are a good many books on how to be efficient and save time. We've written a few ourselves.[1] However, there is a difference between being efficient and being effective. There are three ways to be more effective in the way we spend our life—use our time:

1. Eliminate things we should not be doing (they are not our goals).
2. Do what we should be doing more efficiently.
3. Do the more important things (higher priorities).

Develop a Standard Day

An effective way of managing the details of life is to develop a "standard day" as a basis upon which you might do your planning. In Figure A, we have given a sample standard day for a pastor, an executive and a homemaker. Notice that there are times in each one of these days to reach the goals of the individual and also times left open for the goals of others.

It is very unlikely that there will be many days which will go

Sample Standard Day Homemaker	Sample Standard Day Pastor	Sample Standard Day Executive
7:00 get dressed, prepare breakfast	7:00 Wake up and dress	7:00 Devotion time dress
7:30 breakfast	7:30 Breakfast	7:30 Breakfast
8:00 Kids to school	8:00	8:00 Discuss day with sec'y. Replan day
8:30 Personal devotions	8:30 Review with Sec'y answer mail	8:30 Correspondence
9:00 Plan evening meal	9:00	9:00
9:30	9:30 Study	9:30
10:00 Preliminary dinner preparation	10:00	10:00 Return & Make calls
10:30	10:30 Sermon Work	10:30 Meetings
11:00 open	11:00	11:00
11:30	11:30 Make phone calls	11:30
12:00 Lunch	12:00 open	12:00 Lunch
12:30	12:30	12:30
1:00 open	1:00	1:00
1:30	1:30 Calling	1:30 Open
2:00	2:00	2:00
2:30	2:30	2:30
3:00	3:00 Between calls Office visits	3:00
3:30 Welcome kids home from school.	3:30	3:30
4:00 complete dinner arrangements	4:00	4:00
4:30	4:30	4:30 Plan next day
5:00	5:00 Plan next day	5:00
5:30 Time with husband	5:30	5:30
6:00 Dinner	6:00 Dinner	6:00
6:30	6:30	6:30
7:00 open	7:00 open	7:00
7:30	7:30	7:30
8:00	8:00	8:00
8:30 Kids to bed	8:30	8:30
9:00	9:00	9:00
9:30	9:30	9:30
10:00	10:00	10:00
10:30	10:30	10:30

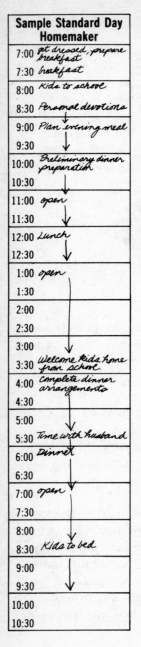
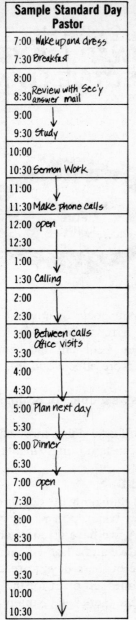
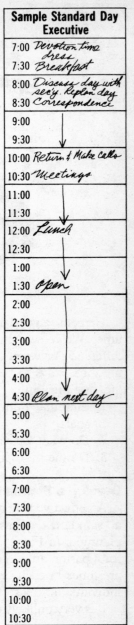

Figure A

exactly like the standard day. That is not the important thing. The advantage in having a standard day is that you have predetermined times during which you will do certain activities. Consequently, you don't have to be continually asking yourself "What do I do next?" or "When should I do this?"

When someone asks you for an appointment or wants to get together with you socially, you have an immediate reference point to which you can refer. The standard day also helps others understand how you operate and when is a good time to get in touch with you. The more others know about you, the more they are likely to be able to fit into *your* life plans.

Consider a Standard Week

There is also a need to have a standard week. There are many things that we do on a weekly basis. The weekend time lends a natural rhythm to life. There are shopping days, reporting days, school days, church days, all of which need to fit into the week.

But there are other things which also need to be put in there, times which can move you toward your life goals. Consider some special family times, such as family weekly planning, discussions on finances, weekly sharing times or outings together. What about weekly times of personal enhancement, courses at school, reading that favorite book, planning to "waste" a whole day doing "nothing"? All these things can help life be more of a whole, give you a sense of knowing where you have been, who you are and where you are going.

Family Planning Time

Too often different members of the family go their own way without communicating to the others their needs and their desires, as well as their goals. We've already indicated how useful the slip technique is in planning vacations (see Chap. 11). But there are many other areas of family life that can be planned using the techniques that we have discussed.

If you have not already thrown out your TV set, you probably continue to wrestle with the problem of TV scheduling. What about deciding on the maximum number of hours that the TV is going to be on within a given week and then using the slip technique to list all of the programs that each member of the family would like to see? Use the ABC technique to sort out which ones should have the highest priority in the family. From this you can develop a TV schedule by circling programs in the TV guide. The rest of the time pull the plug!

The same approach can be taken to the use of the family car or other family equipment. Consider family planning and discussing such subjects as, "What is the purpose of the evening meal together?" "What is the best way for the family to invest its money?" "How can we help each other with our schooling?" "What is the best way of managing the care and maintenance of our home?"

Remember, "Good goals are my goals, and bad goals are your goals," which is another way of saying that shared goals are good goals and imposed goals are bad goals. We are motivated most to do those things which we plan together and decide together. A family has a life of its own. That life also needs a life-goal statement.[2]

"Things-to-Do" List

Earlier we talked about the simple technique of just writing down everything you plan to do the next day. This is a very effective way to begin gaining control over your life and time. There are a number of different notebooks that you can get to do this. There is even one notebook available in stationery stores entitled *Dumb Things I Have to Do.* Some desk and pocket calendars have a place to write things that you should do on a particular day.

Many men and women have found it convenient to design their own "Things-to-Do" list and have it mimeographed or even printed, to their own specifications. An example of what one person did is given in Figure B. Notice that this individual has followed the very valuable principle of *grouping* different kinds of events. Experience has shown that most people like things best when they do them in sequence.

Your Environment

Arrange your environment to fit your goals. There will always be trade-offs in the amount of time that you can invest in doing different things. For example, if you have a lot of brass objects around the house that need to be polished, it might be "cheaper" for you in the long run to have them all polished and sprayed by an expert rather than polishing them yourself. The same would be true of things like yard work.

Essentially what you are doing is trading off money against hours. But since hours are your *life,* they are the most important thing!

The same idea can be true of your trading off and negotiating family time. Time is always compromised. There are *your* needs, *your* goals, and then there are *others'* goals. In all of this keep trying to think of life as a whole rather than as a compartmentalization.

Use Pareto's Principle

Vilfredo Pareto was a brilliant Italian mathematician, sociologist and economist of the last century. He came up with what has come to be known as the 80/20 rule. Simply stated it says that "80 percent of the result will come from 20 percent of the events." In church 80 percent of the work gets done by 20 percent of the people; 80 percent of a company's sales come from 20 percent of its products; 80 percent of the outcome of a football game will be the result of 20 percent of the time spent on the field. To put it another way, using our ABC technique, given ten items only two will be A's.

You can take advantage of this principle by consciously

DAILY PLANNING SHEET

Date_____

Letters to Write

____ Thank-you notes to
____ dinner hosts.
____ Don Jones — re/ Boston
____ trip.
____ _____
____ _____

People to See

____ Warren Lutz
____ John Seward
____ George Hann
____ _____
____ _____
____ _____

Things to Be Done

____ Draft new project pro-
____ posal.
____ Investigate current pro-
____ cedures for educ. mtrls.
____ Thank-you notes to hosts.
____ Memos written on staff
____ mtg.
____ Check out publicity photos.
____ _____

Things to Be Planned

____ New billing procedures.
____ Budget for new fiscal
____ year to be begun
____ _____
____ _____
____ _____

Items to Be Obtained

____ New slide projector,
____ extra carousels.
____ _____
____ _____
____ _____

↑ Write priority in this column

Phone Calls to Make

____ Ray Baker 798-1233
____ R. Dorney 307/772-9423
____ Wife. 458-6460
____ a. Yamkin (check w/
____ information)
____ new address

Appointments

6:00	
6:30	
7:00	
7:30	
8:00	
8:30	Telephoning
9:00	Dictation, Reading mail,
9:30	etc.
10:00	
10:30	
11:00	↓
11:30	
12:00	Lunch w/ Bill & Steve
12:30	to discuss budget &
1:00	billing
1:30	Planning time.
2:00	
2:30	
3:00	
3:30	
4:00	Free time for others.
4:30	
5:00	
5:30	
6:00	
6:30	
7:00	
7:30	Bible Study Fellowship
8:00	Needham's house
8:30	
9:00	
9:30	
10:00	

Figure B

looking for the two opportunities out of ten that will have real payoff, for the two minutes of your time that will save you eight. And reverse the idea: 80 percent of the time that you "waste" (another way of saying you don't like what you're doing) will be caused by only 20 percent of the things you do. Find those 20 percent and eliminate them.

Apply this principle to your planning. What are the two key steps out of the ten that you have to take that will really bring success? Of the next ten meetings that you are supposed to attend, which two are really important?

Turn it around again. Of the ten people who keep requesting time from you, which two are taking 80 percent of your time?

Discern God's Timing

We are trying to uncover God's strategy for our life and become a part of it. We need to be constantly looking for God's timing. Look for that key moment in the life of others when you can really be God's person, God's minister, to them.

Take Advantage of Delays

We spend a great deal of time just waiting for things to happen. If you must wait, wait. But don't fret about it. Put the time to work. Pull out your Life Goals Statement and review that. Carry along a book that you always wanted to read. Review your appointment calendar and go over your priorities.

Look at the world around you and find some new thing that you didn't observe before. Strike up a conversation on a positive subject with a person who is also waiting with you. Carry with you a list or post on the wall of your home things you could do in 10 minutes: change the washer in the leaky faucet, clean one drip pan under a stove burner, write a note of appreciation to a friend.

Use Strategy When You Shop

Just the act of going to a supermarket consumes a great deal

171

of time. Combine as many purchases as you can to save the time of moving from one store to another. Try to arrange your shopping list in the order in which you know you will move through the supermarket. If you make this a habit, after a while you won't even need the list.

Shop during times when the stores aren't crowded, such as directly after dinner. Carry the current sizes of your children's clothes with you, so that when you see a clothing bargain you can take advantage of it. Buy in quantity whenever you can.

Have a Strategy for Cleaning the House

Do your sweeping first so that you don't lay dust on tables you've just dusted. Work to have mats that will pick up the mud at the doors. Stretch out your "spring cleaning" over a number of days by making a list of one thing or one room which you will do on a certain day. Perhaps one day you will shampoo the rugs, and another day, wax the hardwood floors.

Cut down on your laundry time by buying clothes that require little ironing and don't run easily. Read labels on both the clothes and the laundry detergents. Make sure that the family isn't using the laundry hamper as a place to deposit clean clothes rather than hang them up. Ask everyone in the family to find their own clothes after they've been laundered and dried and do their own sorting. On washday have everyone take his own sheets off the bed and put on clean ones.

How Clergymen Misuse Their Time

Charles Reimnitz, a Lutheran who has presented a number of seminar workshops for professional groups, has focused on "The Dirty Dozen: Time Wasters for Clergymen."[2]

Here are Reimnitz's "Dirty Dozen":
1. Personal disorganization
2. Problems with delegation
3. Interruptions
4. Indecision and procrastination

172

5. Socializing
6. Junk mail and outside reading
7. Lack of planning
8. Television
9. Meetings
10. Family problems and family errands
11. Traveling time and car problems
12. Fatigue

These time wasters pretty well agree with what we have discovered in our own Managing Your Time seminars. Make up your own list and go to work on it.

Time Is Life

It really is. We'll try to sum it up in the next chapter.

Footnotes

1. There are many good books on time management. Some of the most current include Ed Dayton's *Tools for Time Management* (Grand Rapids: Zondervan, 1974), Ted W. Engstrom and Alex MacKenzie's *Managing Your Time* (Grand Rapids: Zondervan, 1967) and Alan Lakein's *How to Get Control of Your Time and Your Life.* One of the "originals" that is still around is Laird's *The Technique of Getting Things Done* (New York: McGraw-Hill, 1947). But remember, all the tools in the world won't help you if you are working toward the wrong goal!

2. For a good understanding of how families interact among their members, see Nathan Ackerman's *The Psychodynamics of Family Life* (New York: Basic Books, 1958).

CHAPTER 17

TIME IS LIFE

What we need for a strategy for Christian living are goals, priorities and planning. But what about the time to do all this? What about life? Time is both immensely valuable and utterly irretrievable. It is undoubtedly the most valuable commodity we have.

We so often hear, "I wish I knew how to manage my time better." Rarely do we hear, "I wish I knew how to manage myself better." To manage our lives we must then obviously learn to manage ourselves. Actually good time management is the only way we can possibly get more time for the things we *really* want to do.

Where Does the Time Go?

We all ask the question, "Where has the time gone?" This rhetorical question certainly misstates the case. Time does not depart the scene; it simply passes at the rate it always has—while we accomplish far less than perhaps we should have.

Better to ask, "How could I have planned so poorly and left so much to be done in so little time?"

Time can be lost but it can never be retrieved. It cannot be hoarded; it must be spent. Someone has said that we cannot rent, hire or buy time. We cannot store it, freeze it or can it. We cannot manufacture it. Time is perhaps the only talent that every human being is equally responsible for. (Note Matt. 25 and the parable of the talents.)

Much is said and preached in our Christian circles regarding the stewardship of wealth and possessions. Less, possibly, is said about the stewardship of talents which God has given us. Very little is said concerning our stewardship of time. Possibly it is even less understood. However, we believe that Scripture indicates each of us as believers will be held accountable for our use of time as we stand before the Lord in eternity—when time is no more.

The apostle Paul in Colossians 4:5 says: "Make the best possible use of your time" (*Phillips*). Again, in Ephesians 5:15 and 16 Paul says: "Live life, then, with a due sense of responsibility, not as men who do not know the meaning and purpose of life but as *those who do*. Make the best use of your time, despite all the difficulties of these days."

No One Has More Time Than You

No one has any more—or any less—time than you do and we do. To each of us is given 1440 minutes of every day, 168 hours per week. We all have the same amount of time in every day as does everyone else. Here is the paradox: No one has enough time; everyone has all the time there is.

Even our Lord Jesus Christ, the Word who was made flesh and dwelt among us, lived in a very short span of time of only 33½ years. Yet think of the *quality* of His time and investment!

Yet in spite of its recognized preciousness and vast potentiality, there is nothing we squander quite so thoughtlessly as time. It was the wise and pragmatic Sir Walter Scott who wrote:

> "Dost thou love life?
>   Then do not squander time,
>   For that's the stuff life is made of."

Each of us should think of time as being the raw material of life itself. Every day brings to each of us the opportunity to evolve into something better than we were at the start of the day. The apostle Peter says that we are to "grow in the grace and in the knowledge of our Lord and Saviour Jesus Christ" (2 Pet. 3:18, *NEB*). This growth in grace and knowledge takes place within a time span, within *life*.

Be Successful

Our personal success, or the lack of it, is largely contingent upon the effective use of the time given to us. All of us should strive to be "successful." There is nothing really meritorious in being unsuccessful—provided, as we have indicated in the earlier chapters, that our goals are right.

Success is a good word—not a bad word. By success we do not necessarily mean always reaching a goal. As we have indicated, some people go through life thinking they have never had a failure because they have reached every goal. But the truth is they have set their goals so safely low that they couldn't possibly miss them!

On the other hand, there are those who think that they have had failures in life when really they haven't. They have strived, not always successfully, to reach their maximum—and after all, that is what success really boils down to. Success is not always a matter of reaching every goal. Nor is it a matter of eliminating problems. Success is achieving the maximum of the potential that is available to us at a given point in time.

Time Seems to Have Strange Qualities

It extends in the first week of a vacation and contracts in the second. It is slower for the patient than for the dentist. It is

177

slower for the congregation than for the preacher. It is slower for the student than for the teacher.

We have been told that time goes by. It does not; we go by. Time stands still. Time is *now*. The only time we have is now. This is the existential quality of time.

For all of us, and particularly for the Christian, there is an urgency attached to time. Our Lord Jesus felt it when He said: "I must work the works of him that sent me, while it is day: the night cometh, when no man can work" (John 9:4).

The pioneer missionary, Robert Moffatt, certainly felt it when he wrote: "We shall have all eternity in which to celebrate our victories, but we have only one short hour before the sunset in which to win them."

Time Really Is but a Measurement, a Dimension

Thus, time in itself can scarcely be our problem. When we look into the matter of time and its management, and the management of life, all roads ultimately lead back to the management of ourselves.

Our supply of time is totally perishable. The only variable available to us is the use we make of our finite supply of time. Thus we need to budget the time we have to spend, just as carefully as we budget the money we have to spend. Time's business calls for a budget. There is a time to pray and a time to play. The time-thrifty Christian neglects neither, uses both. Remember that time really can be our tool—and we need not be its slave.

Peter Drucker, prominent management authority, has stated: "Time management takes perseverance and self-discipline—but no other investment pays higher dividends."

Time Is Saved by Discipline

Time is not saved by multiplying devices. It is saved by personal discipline. It is the person, not the mechanics, that will make the difference. Imposing deadlines and exercising self-discipline will aid us in overcoming indecision, vacillation and procrastination. Again, quoting Mr. Drucker, "Nothing so much distinguishes effective executives as their tender loving care of time."

The famed British scholar, Professor C. Northcote Parkinson, has given us several laws, the first of which is, "Work expands so as to fill whatever time is available for it." This "law" is not just an entertaining bit of nonsense. Any executive who has not observed this law at work in his own behavior and that of his associates and subordinates has been living with his eyes closed.

Mr. Drucker says that "those executives who really get things done don't start with their work; they start with their time." What is he saying? He is saying that the effective person in managing his life carves time out of his calendar and uses his time to be creative and to take the initiative. He does not simply and continually react to the pressures of the hour or of the day. Drucker stresses that the effective executive is the one who uses his time creatively to do the things he *really wants to do*.

Given two executives of equal ability, the one who plans his or her time more effectively will vastly out-perform the other. He or she will make time for creative thinking and problem solving which are vital to the job. The second will put them off until he "finds time." The same is true of the homemaker or the college student, the head of the church committee or the building custodian.

Time Must Be Spent

All of us have said from time to time that "time is money and must be spent wisely." However, we have no choice not to spend it. The question is how wisely are we spending it. We may "stop the clock" on the basketball court or the football field but never in the game of life. Yesterday is a cancelled check; tomorrow is simply a promissory note. Today must be spent wisely.

Ask Questions

The kind of questions we ought to be asking ourselves in this matter of managing our time and life would be, for example:

What am I now doing that does not need to be done by me or anyone else? Perhaps this task or these responsibilities ought to be eliminated.

What am I now doing that should be done by someone else? Perhaps much of what we are doing can and ought to be delegated.

What am I now doing that wastes my time or other people's time?

There are two major ways of saving time. The first is to do things more effectively. The second is to eliminate those things that we should not be doing.

Learn to Set "Posteriorities"

Setting individual priorities is simply a matter of deciding what you want to do and when you want to do it. But we also need to set "posteriorities"—deciding what tasks not to tackle and sticking to that decision. You perhaps have noted, as we have, that what you postpone, you usually abandon.

As Dr. Richard C. Halverson has indicated, "Priorities are not just marginal options . . . they are life determining. One's personality is molded inescapably into the image of his priorities."

The effective Christian must have an ambition to excel and honor Christ in all that he does. He must be able to select—set priorities. He must be able to reject—set "posteriorities."

One Thing at a Time

Some people seem to be able to accomplish a great deal more than others. What is their secret? Often their approach is to do things one at a time according to their priorities. Doing things one at a time helps them accomplish their task much faster than if they tried to do many things at once. In other words, they concentrate, they set priorities and stick to them. Remember—it is not how much we do that counts, but how much we get done!

There are enough hours in each day for each of us to fulfill God's perfect and particular plan for our lives.

Take time to work—it is the price of success.

Take time to think—it is the source of power.

Take time to play—it is the secret of perpetual youth.

Take time to read—it is the fountain of wisdom.

Take time to be friendly—it is a road to happiness.

Take time to dream—it is hitching your wagon to a star.

Take time to love and be loved—it is the privilege of redeemed people.

Take time to look around—it is too short a day to be selfish.

Take time to laugh—it is the music of the soul.

Take time for God—it is life's only lasting investment.

—Author Unknown

CHAPTER 18

YOU HAVE A STRATEGY
FOR LIVING

What we have offered in these pages is no simple formula. We don't promise that you will immediately become happy or wealthy or even "successful," but we do believe you will find here an approach to a total Christian life-style that will make you a more effective and God-honoring person.

This is a way of thinking about life, a *strategy* for living.

This is a way of encountering life with an inner direction, a Holy Spirit empowered motivation. It is not the only approach to life or thinking about life, but it is one that is particularly suitable for the Christian who is constantly pushed and pulled by a Western technological society.

In the circular diagram that appears throughout the book, we have tried to indicate that all this is a process.

Set Goals

We need to begin by setting goals. Goals are motivators. They not only give direction, but they supply the drive and desire.

Establish Priorities

Setting goals leads to the need for priorities. When we recognize that we need priorities, we are forced to examine our value system and, as Christians, go back to the Bible for underlying principles. This is not an easy task. It is a task which requires a continual review to make sure that we are not being swayed by the culture or that our biblical interpretation is not a cultural interpretation.

Make Plans

High priority goals need plans. Plans are really anticipated actions taken within specified time periods. In other words, they are a schedule of activities. Somehow these should fit into our schedule, our calendars and appointment books.

Develop Schedules

Schedules are the steps toward goals. They are the detailed plans. A plan should result in our achieving a goal, and this immediate goal should be part of some life goal which should fit into our total life purpose.

Anticipate Problems

Still, we need to realize that life will never be exactly what we expect. The best of plans will encounter unexpected *problems.*

Suppose our goal is to have a vacation together as a family. Problems may force us to do several things, but we can always work around the problems by changing our schedule, replanning or changing our priorities.

For example, our car gets a flat tire, causing us to *change our schedule.* We arrive at our vacation destination two hours late.

Or, our car has a major breakdown. The repair bill eats up all our vacation funds. We have to *replan* our vacation—where we will go, when we can leave.

Or, as we leave town for our vacation we have a minor automobile accident and our youngest daughter needs minor emergency first aid. We *change our priorities* and see to our daughter's welfare before getting back on the road.

All these problems can force us to change our schedules, change our plans, or even change our immediate priorities. None of these problems, however, need change the original goal of sharing a week together on vacation as a family.

Problems should be seen as a deviation from your goal. If when you encounter a problem, you can't identify any goal which is being hindered by your failure to overcome this problem, that's a good indication that perhaps the goal should take a low priority on your ABC list.

Utilize New Information

On the other hand, *new information* can have an impact on not only your schedule, plans and priorities, but also your goals. The announcement that your oldest daughter has won an educational trip to Europe may completely change your goal to spend a vacation together.

As we *expect* life to work this way, we will find that we gain a greater ability to keep steering, to stay in the middle of the stream.

Don't Be a "Time Nut"

Whatever you do, don't get "uptight" about this matter of time management. Remember, time is to work for us. So let's not get a guilt complex over it.

None of us wants to become a "time nut." Such people are definitely not pleasant to be around. They are constantly checking their watches, making time schedules for themselves, revising the schedules, acting nervous and jittery about wasting time (and perhaps writing books to tell other people how important time is!).

And Don't Be a "Goal Nut"

As you seek to avoid being a time nut, beware also of becoming a "goal nut." You don't have to be thinking about goals, goals, goals, goals every minute, hour and day. Review your goals from time to time—perhaps once a week will be plenty for you. Check your progress in reaching your goals, then go about the business of living until the next review. Remember that the strategy outlined in this book is supposed to be a *process,* not a prison.

Control Your Time

Getting control of your time does not require that you become a "time nut." That is over-controlling your time. You soon become obsessed with it.

The idea behind controlling your time is that you work smarter, not harder. The more control we have over our time, the freer we will feel to do all of the things we really want to do.

That freedom is gained by controls is a paradoxical statement but that is why we need to plan. Perhaps one of the easiest ways to understand it is to think about stop lights within a city. Traffic lights control our movements as we drive through the streets.

On the other hand, if there were no traffic lights, it would take us five times longer to get across the city. So it is that as we set in checkpoints, planning points, goal setting times within our lives and begin to control our lives with reference to these, we gain new freedom to be what we ought to be and do what we ought to do.

Plan for Life Planning

Take an immediate step right now, no matter how small. But, at the same time, don't try to do it all at once. Within the next 24 hours, schedule some time to do your initial Life Goal Statement. Make a date with yourself! Set aside two or three hours on your calendar now. Plan to do your Time Inventory sometime within the next month to six weeks.

Meanwhile, you can be taking a look at the Time Commitment Sheet and making a list of commitments that you now have. You can carry these around with you and make additions during those "spare moments" that always seem to be cropping up.

Plan to start working on your long-range goals within a month, on your medium-range goals within two weeks and on your short-range goals within a week.

Put some time down on your calendar three months from now when you're going to spend an afternoon or an evening reviewing everything that has transpired so far. Be ready to change your goals.

Look forward to the day, perhaps six to twelve months from now, when you will repeat the entire process again.

In all of this keep a healthy tension between the fact that God does the leading, but you do the planning.

And remember that in every day there is always enough time to do the perfect will of God.

One of the great liberating truths related to life and its management is that there are enough hours in each day for each of us to fulfill God's perfect and particular plan for our lives. We never need more time than we have to do the whole will of God.

As the late Adlai Stevenson said: "It is not the days of your life, but the life in your days that counts."

So as you seek a strategy for Christian living, "Live life, then, with a due sense of responsibility, not as men who do not know the meaning and purpose of life but as *those who do*. Make the best use of your time, despite all the difficulties of these days."

BIBLIOGRAPHY

Ackerman, Nathan W. *The Psychodynamics of Family Life.* New York: Basic Books Inc., 1958.

Allport, Gordon W. *Becoming: Basic Considerations for a Psychology of Personality.* New Haven: Yale University Press, 1955.

_____. *Pattern and Growth in Personality.* New York: Holt, Rinehart and Winston Inc., 1961.

Bolles, Richard. *What Color Is Your Parachute?* New York: Crown Publishers Inc., 1973.

Churchman, C. West. *The Systems Approach.* New York: Dell Books, 1969.

Dayton, Edward R. *God's Purpose/Man's Plans.* Monrovia, CA: MARC, 1972.

_____. *Tools for Time Management.* Grand Rapids: Zondervan Publishing House, 1974.

Dobson, James, *Hide or Seek*. Old Tappan, NJ: Fleming H. Revell Co., 1974.

Drucker, Peter F. *The Age of Discontinuity: Guidelines to Changing Our Society*. New York: Harper and Row Publishers, Inc., 1969.

Engstrom, Ted W., and Dayton, Ed R. *The Art of Management for Christian Leaders*. Waco, TX: Word Inc., 1976.

Engstrom, Ted W. and MacKenzie, Alex. *Managing Your Time*. Grand Rapids: Zondervan Publishing House, 1958.

Getz, Gene A. *Sharpening the Focus of the Church*. Chicago: Moody Press, 1974.

Ginott, Haim G. *Between Parent & Child*. New York: Avon Books, 1973.

Hersey, Paul, and Blanchard, Kenneth H. *Management of Organization Behavior*. Englewood Cliffs, NJ: Prentice-Hall Inc., 1969.

Johnson, Ben E. *Rapid Reading with a Purpose*. Ventura, CA Regal Books, 1973.

Johnson, David W., and Johnson, Frank P. *Joining Together*. Englewood Cliffs, NJ: Prentice-Hall Inc., 1975.

Kennedy, Gerald. *The Lion and the Lamb*. Nashville: Abingdon, 1950.

Kepner, Charles H., and Tregoe, B.B. *The Rational Manager*. New York: McGraw-Hill Book Co., 1965.

Kiev, Ari. *A Strategy for Daily Living*. New York: Free Press, 1973.

Lakein, Alan. *How to Get Control of Your Time and Your Life*. New York: Peter H. Wyden, Inc., 1973.

Lewin, Kurt. *Field Theory in Social Science*. Cartwright Dorwin, ed. Westport, CT: Greenwood PRess, 1975.

Mager, Robert. *Goal Analysis*. Belmont, CA: Fearon Publishers, Inc., 1972.

Maslow, Abraham H. *Motivation and Personality*. New York: Harper and Row Publishers Inc., 1954.

Miller, Keith. *The Becomers*. Waco, TX: Word, Inc., 1973.

Mollenkott, Virginia R. *In Search of Balance*. Waco, TX: Word Inc., 1969.

Mooneyham, Stanley. *What Do You Say to a Hungry World?* Waco, TX: Word, Inc., 1975.

Neighbour, Ralph W. Jr. *The Seven Last Words of the Church: We Never Did It That Way Before*. Grand Rapids: Zondervan Publishing House, 1973.

O'Connor, Elizabeth, *Journey Inward, Journey Outward*. New York: Harper and Row Publishers, Inc., 1968.

Ortlund, Raymond C. *Lord, Make My Life a Miracle*. Ventura, CA: Regal Books, 1974.

Osgood, Don. *The Family and the Corporation Man*. New York: Harper and Row Publishers, Inc., 1975.

Ramm, Bernard L. *The Right, the Good, and the Happy*. Waco, TX: Word, Inc., 1971.

Reimnitz, Charles. "How Clergymen Use (Misuse) Their Time." *Church Management*. March, 1975.

Simon, Sidney, et al. *Values Clarification*. New York: Hart Publishing Co., 1972.

Slater, Philip E. *Pursuit of Loneliness*. Boston: Beacon Press, 1971.

Wright, H. Norman. *Communication: Key to Your Marriage*. Ventura, CA: Regal Books, 1974.

Morgan, Marabel. *The Total Woman*. Old Tappan, NJ: Revell, 1973.

MoMaynard, Stanley. *What Do I Want to Say to a Hurting World?* Waco, TX: Word, Inc., 1978.

Neighbour, Ralph W., Jr. *The Seven Last Words of the Church*. R. Vencer, D., & Carey, W., Jr. Grand Rapids: Zondervan Publishing House, 1974.

Orlando, Elizabeth. *Successful Women, American Style*. New York: Harper and Row Publishers, Inc., 1978.

Ortlund, Raymond C. *Lord, Make My Life a Miracle*. Ventura, CA: Regal Books, 1974.

Ortlund, Ruth. *The Family Under the Corporation Blues*. New York: Harper and Row Publishers, Inc., 1979.

Pippin, Bernard F. *The High and Holy One*. Fort Worth: Word, TX: Word Inc., 1974.

Redman, Lange. *Peace Conspiracy, Our Christian Illness*. New Orleans: Wendy, Scott & Sons, 1974.

Small, Dwight. *After You've Said I Do*. New York: Fleming H. Revell Co., 1973.

Strauss, William F. *The Art of Communication*. Eugene: Herald Press, 1971.

Wright, H. Norman. *Communication: Key to Your Marriage*. Ventura, CA: Regal Books, 1974.